Turnstones 2

An English course for Scotland

Allicia Coates

Brian Fitzpatrick

Sheila Hughes

Alan Keay

Editors:

Sheila Hughes

Gordon Liddell

Series editor:

Robbie Robertson

Hodder & Stoughton

A MEMBER OF THE HODDER HEADLINE GROUP

Acknowledgements

The publishers would like to thank the following individuals, institutions and companies for permission to reproduce photographs in this book. Every effort has been made to trace ownership of copyright. The publishers would be happy to make arrangements with any copyright holder whom it has not been possible to contact.

Action Plus (128 top); Corbis (48 photos one, five and six, 102 top two and bottom left); Hulton Archive (48 photo three); Life File (48 photo eight, 62, 123, 128 bottom); Natural History Museum (4); Ronald Grant (48 photo four, 50, 53); PA Photos (44, 102 bottom right); Photodisc (122, 123); SNSPIX (48 photos two and seven, 64 both); Topham/UUP (81).

**In memory of Robbie Robertson,
Series Editor for Turnstones.**

Orders: please contact Bookpoint Ltd, 130 Milton Park, Abingdon, Oxon OX14 4SB. Telephone: (44)01235 827720, Fax: (44) 01235 400454. Lines are open from 9.00–6.00, Monday to Saturday, with a 24 hour message anwering service. Email address: orders@bookpoint.co.uk

British Library Cataloguing in Publication Data
A catalogue record for this title is available from The British Library

ISBN 0 340 79037 7

First published 2002
Impression number   10 9 8 7 6 5 4 3 2 1
Year   2008 2007 2006 2005 2004 2003 2002

Copyright @ 2002 Allicia Coates, Brian Fitzpatrick, Sheila Hughes, Alan Keay, Gordon Liddell, Robbie Robertson

Cover photo from David Rudkin
Typeset by Fakenham Photosetting Limited, Fakenham, Norfolk
Printed in Italy for Hodder & Stoughton Educational, a division of Hodder Headline Plc, 338 Euston Road, London NW1 3BH.

Contents

About Turnstones 2   4

Using Turnstones 2   5

1 Unlocking the text   7

2 Language as communication   9

Unlocking your imagination
3 Cover stories   11
4 Story lines   17
5 Characters   22
6 Other story features   26
7 Scots voices: monologue   31
8 Scots voices: dialogue   36

Fun challenge
9 Found poems   39

Unlocking the text: Mass media
10 Photographs and posters   47
11 Film   59
12 Newspapers   64

Fun challenge
13 Neologisms   73

Information
14 Unlocking the treasure chest: reading for information   79

15 Unlocking the treasure chest: stage 1 – preparing for the trip   85

16 Unlocking the treasure chest: stage 2 – where to find interesting information   89

17 Unlocking the treasure chest: stage 3 – deciding what treasure to bring home   93

18 Unlocking the treasure chest: stage 4 – presenting what you have found to your audience   100

Unlocking persuasion
19 Sooking up and sounding off   105
20 Hard facts and sound sources   112

Fun challenge
21 Unlocking signs   122

Unlocking talk
22 It's not what you say, it's the way that you say it   124

Unlocking writing
23 It's not what you write, it's the way that you write it   138

Unlocking presentation
24 Showing your best face: punctuation   151

Unlocking presentation
25 Showing your best face: layout   156

Glossary   161

About Turnstones 2

We began **Turnstones 1** by explaining to you that it was named after a bird which turns stones over to look for good things underneath. Hopefully, you found some good things as you dipped in and out of the book.

What are you going to find in Turnstones 2?

Hopefully more things to interest you. We are going to begin **Turnstones 2** with a look at another bird. This one is called a dodo but unfortunately it no longer exists. It is extinct.

Why do you think this happened?

Here is one theory.

The Dodo, 1598–1681

In the year 1598 AD, Portuguese sailors landing on the shores of the island of Mauritius discovered a previously unknown species of bird, the dodo. The dodo had been totally isolated – it could not fly and had never been off the island. The dodo greeted the new visitors with a child-like innocence. The sailors mistook the gentle spirit of the dodo, and its lack of fear of humans, as stupidity. They called the bird 'dodo' (meaning something similar to a simpleton in the Portuguese language). Many dodos were killed by the human visitors, and those that survived attacks from man had to face the animals they had brought with them. Dogs and pigs, which soon became wild when introduced to the Mauritian eco-system, killed the dodo for food. By the year 1681, the last dodo had died, and the world was left worse with its passing.

So what's this got to do with **Turnstones 2**? If you never step out of your own surroundings, and if you take everyone and everything at face value – as the dodo did – you might as well be extinct too! We want you to look around and keep turning things over like a turnstone.

pages 91–92 You can find out more about the dodo on http://www.davidreilly.com/dodo/

Using Turnstones 2

As in *Turnstones 1*, we don't expect you to begin at page 1 and work all the way through to the last page. You and your teacher will decide which bits you want to dip into, but we would like you to work through Chapters 1 and 2 before you begin jumping about.

Sometimes you will work as a whole team: your teacher and the rest of the class. Sometimes you will work with a smaller team of two, three or four other pupils. Sometimes you will work with one special partner and sometimes you will be on your own, but you will always have support around you: from the book; your teacher; your classmates and members of your family. Don't forget to use the support!

In the margin of a lot of pages you'll find icons – special marks with particular meanings. Below you will find a list of these icons with the explanations of what they mean.

You'll also see, from time to time, that a word has been printed in a different colour. This tells you that the meaning of the word can be found perhaps in a panel in the margin, and certainly in the Glossary on pages 161 to 166. Like a dictionary the Glossary is alphabetically arranged.

Glossary

Dictionary
A book listing words in alphabetical order, giving their meanings, how they are said and sometimes their histories.

ICONS	MEANINGS
pages 0-0	Later parts of *Turnstones 2* at page(s) such-and-such can be connected to this section or part of a section.
pages 0-0	Earlier parts of *Turnstones 2* at page(s) such-and-such can be connected to this section or part of a section.
	Extract will be available on the internet at www.turnstones-online.co.uk

1 Unlocking the text

Glossary

Communication
The exchange of information, ideas and feelings between individuals and groups.

Turnstones is a series about communication. How do we communicate with each other in the twenty-first century? Look at the picture below and, working with a partner, see how many different forms of communication you can find.

Can you think of any other methods of communication, which we have missed in this picture? Discuss this with the rest of the class. Did some people come up with things you didn't think of? Try the task again with the next picture and see if you find it easier this time.

Glossary

Text
Any made thing which conveys information e.g. writing, pictures, recorded conversation, sound, etc.

You will have worked out that there are many, many ways in which we communicate with one another. Some of these involve reading and writing, talking and listening (in other words language); but some of them don't. What is the baby in the pram communicating when he is crying? What are the young couple communicating when they are walking along hand in hand, saying nothing?

We have called this first chapter 'Unlocking the text'. The '**text**', in this case, is two illustrations of how people communicate. Just as you unlock a box to get at its contents, we can unlock a text to get at its meaning. To unlock the meaning of the illustrations you have used your eyes, experience and wits. But most of the 'texts' in this book have their meanings locked up in the language of stories, poems and other forms of writing. To unlock them, you need special knowledge and skills. And we are going to have fun teaching you this special knowledge and these skills.

2 Language as communication

Glossary

Audience
The person or persons reading, watching or listening to a text (see target audience).

Purpose
The main intention or reason for doing something. In this case for writing or talking in a particular way.

Now we are going to focus more on how we communicate using language. We want you to understand how some people use language to have power over you and to influence the way you think and feel. We also want you to have power and control over the language you use and to realise how you can change your language for a variety of **audiences** and **purposes**.

Do you think you should change the way you speak in different situations? Read what Liz Lochhead has to say in her poem.

What do you think she is saying about school and the way we speak and write. Talk with a partner about this and then have a class discussion.

Kidspoem/ Bairnsang

It wiz January
and a gey dreich day
the first day I went to the school
so
ma Mum happed me up in ma good navyblue nap coat
wi the rid tartan hood
birled a scarf aroon ma neck
pu'ed on ma pixie anpawkies
it wis that bitter
said
'noo ye'll no starve'
gied me a wee kiss and kidoan skelp on the bum
and sent me off across the playground
to the place I'd learn to say
'It was January
and a really dismal day
the first day I went to school
so
my Mother wrapped me up in my best navyblue top coat
with the red tartan hood
twirled a scarf around my neck
pulled on my bobble-hat and mittens
it was so bitterly cold
said
'now you won't freeze to death'

gave me a little kiss and pretend slap on the bottom
and sent me off across the playground
to the place I'd learn to forget to say
'It wiz January
and a gey dreich day
the first day I went to the school
so
ma Mum happed me up in ma good navyblue nap coat
wi the rid tartan hood
birled a scarf aroon ma neck
pu'ed on ma pawkies
it wis that bitter'

Oh,
saying it was one thing
but when it came to writing it
in black and white
the way it had to be said
was as if you were posh, grown up, male, English and dead.

By **Liz Lochhead**

Now work in a group of three and decide how you would read this poem out loud. Each of you should take a section of the poem. How are you going to divide the poem up? Who is going to read what parts? How are you going to read them?

page 129

Once you have read it out loud, think some more about what you think Liz Lochhead is saying about the way we speak to different audiences. Do you agree with her?

In this poem the pressure is on the child to change her language as she moves from home to school. We think she needs to keep both languages so that she is bilingual. She needs to be confident in both and to know when it is appropriate to use each language. This book will help **you** to learn which language to use and when.

Glossary

Bilingual
Able to speak, and write in two languages.

3 Unlocking your imagination: cover stories

Book covers are big business. Think about it. What is the first thing you see when you walk into a library or a bookshop? Rows and rows of book covers. The question is, what are book covers for?

The answer to this question will help you to decide why publishers put certain things on book covers. You need to be able to unlock the text of a book cover too.

Work in pairs. Do this exercise without a book in front of you.

What are the following things and where can you find them on a book?

- Blurb
- Spine
- ISBN
- Barcode
- Title
- Publisher's logo

Now look at a book cover (this one will do!) and see if you can spot each of the features listed. If you are stuck ask your teacher to point them out.

What are book covers for?

Book covers are usually made of stiff card and one of their functions is to protect the book inside. But a cover also has to make you want to buy the book. In some ways it works very like an advert for the book.

> **Glossary**
>
> **Target audience**
> The particular audience at which a text is being aimed.

The cover has to appeal to a certain **target audience**. It has to give enough information to persuade someone from that audience to pick it up from amongst all of the others on the shelf and then to buy it. It does this by having attractive pictures on the front and by having a **blurb**, usually on the back cover.

Book covers are all very different.

Find four examples of different kinds of book selected from the following list:

- Junior fiction

- Senior fiction

- Non-fiction, e.g. a textbook or instruction manual

- Autobiography

- Reference

- Catalogue

- Telephone directory

> **Glossary**
>
> **Autobiography**
> The story of a person's life, told by him or herself.
>
> **Characteristics**
> The features of someone or something which are similar to or different from others of the same type.

Bring the books you found back to your table and, in your groups, discuss the main similarities and differences between the *front* covers. One person should make a list of the main **characteristics** of each cover.

For each *front* cover answer the following questions:

1 Who is this book aimed at and how do you know this?

2 What is this book about?

3 How does the front cover catch your attention?

4 What kind of information does the front cover give you? Is it helpful in making you decide if you want to read it?

5 If not, how would you change it?

Fiction book covers

If you don't think that book covers are important look at these two. Same book, same author, same title, different cover. Which cover would be more likely to make you buy the book? Why?

Here are some more book covers. Who do you think the target audience is for each one? How do you know this?

    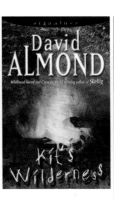 

Glossary

Blurb
Usually appears on the back cover of a book, it is a brief introduction to the subject of the book.

Here, and on the next page, are the **blurbs** which appear on the backs of the books. Can you match them up with their front covers?

Meet Daisy Morelli – a magnet for trouble and a master plotter. When things go wrong – and they always do – who gets the blame? Definitely Daisy!

Daisy's fed up with being told off after a bad day at school. She plans to run away – with best friend Jimmy in tow. They want to join the new soccer academy, chucking in boring lessons for footballing stardom, but teachers pet Winona has other ideas . . .

My life is one of those good news, bad news jokes. I could go on about my good news for hours, but you probably want to hear the punchline. My bad news right? First off my parents got divorced 10 years ago because of me. My dad didn't divorce my mother, or my sister Cindy, or my brother Paul. He divorced me. He couldn't handle my condition so he had to leave. My condition? Well, that brings us to the guts of the bad news.

Shawn has cerebral palsy, no control over his muscles, no hope of improvement, yet humour, joy and love sit alongside frustration in Shawn's mind. His internal life is full of unseen pleasures. But his father perceives only the devastation of an uninhabited body. And Shawn suspects that as his father's sorrow builds, so does his desire to act . . .

They thought we had disappeared, and they were wrong. They thought we were dead, and they were wrong. We stumbled together out of the ancient darkness into the shining valley. The sun glared down on us. The whole world glistened with ice and snow . . .

Who could have known that we would walk together with such happiness, after all we'd been through? It started with a game . . .

In Stoneygate there was a wilderness, an empty space between the house and the river where the ancient coal pit had once been. In the wilderness Kit met Askew, with his wild dog, Jax. Askew – who ran the game called Death.

The wilderness where Kit begins to confront death – and life . . .

When Bella arrives to stay with the Fosters, Abi and Sam are determined to be nice to her. Bella's dad is very ill – it must be awful – POOR Bella!

But it's hard to be sympathetic when Bella is SUCH a boaster. Her parents, her house – even her pedigree pets are BETTER than Abi and Sam's! The girls are trying so hard to be tolerant, but sooner or later something's got to give.

It's been months since Paul has seen his younger brother, Sam. Now Sam has disappeared. Why?

The truth lies at the heart of Watertown; a polluted slum afloat in the city's harbour, where Sam has been working as a research assistant. Paul goes there to find his brother – and encounters people who will stop at nothing to deter him in his quest. Can he and his new friends overcome them – or will the dead water zone overpower everyone who dares to enter it?

Wibbly Pig is very excited about the parcels he has to open.

How does the front cover and the blurb together try to persuade you to read any of these books? Why did they catch your attention?

- Now you have had a chance to look at some blurbs, how do you think they are written?

- How are they different from a summary of the story?

- What kind of words do the blurb-writers use?

Here are three front covers. Choose one and try to make up a blurb to go with the book.

On the next page you will find the actual blurbs.

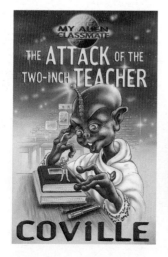

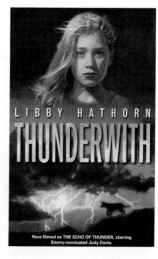

Pleskit's new in school. He's also purple, bald and has a single stalk growing out of the top of his head! It's going to be an interesting first term...

Pleskit's the class alien. He's slowly beginning to settle in at school – with the help of his friend Tim. But when he accidentally manages to shrink the teacher *and* his new best friend, things seem to be going from bad to worse. He has to get them back to normal before anyone finds out – or before anyone steps on them!

Mandy Hope loves animals and knows lots about them too. Both her parents are vets, so Mandy's always able to help her friends with their pet problems...

Mandy has lots of friends with guinea pigs and together they form a gang. But Lisa won't join in with her pedigree guinea pig. Why is she being so snooty?

Lara's parents are divorced and she hardly remembers her father. But when her mother dies, he takes her to live with him, deep in the Australian outback.

Living far away from all that has ever been familiar, Lara feels like an intruder in her father's new family, and fears she will never find love and acceptance.

Until she meets Thunderwith, a mysterious dog who comes and goes, and offers her an unexpected friendship – and the strength to go on...

Which blurb do you prefer – and why? Remember the purpose of the writing and the target audience.

Paired activity

Maybe the English department and the Art department could work together on this challenge.

Imagine you are about to design a cover for the book outlined below. Look at the details given and design an appropriate cover for it.

You must decide on the following aspects and justify your choice for each:

● **Target audience**

● Colour/s for the cover

● Picture/s

● Font type (see the section on layout, page 156, for more ideas about fonts).

page 156

Glossary

Genre
A particular type of text which has features in common with others of the same type.

Title: *The Empty Room*
Author: You
Genre: Thriller

Plot summary: a 14-year-old called Tamara wants to live on her own after her mother's death. She has to avoid being taken into care. As a result, she has to think up a believable story about what has happened to her mother and she has to persuade lots of adults that she can manage on her own.

Remember that this is just a *summary* of the plot. It doesn't make a very attractive blurb. Writing that is up to you.

The next time you go to buy a book or borrow one from the library, look more closely at the cover and think about how it is trying to persuade you to read it. Happy reading!

4 Unlocking your imagination: story lines

Glossary

Narrative
A text which tells a story, e.g. a novel, an opera, a TV soap opera.

Recount
A type of narrative writing telling about past events.

Character
Person or being in a fictional text; his or her personality.

Stories belong to a particular genre known as narrative or recount. This is writing in which the author is *recounting* or *retelling* events for a particular purpose.

- It might be that the author wants his or her audience to feel sorry for or to envy the main character.

- He or she might want to entertain their readers by frightening them or making them laugh.

- They might want to share an experience they have had; something which meant a lot to them.

Real writers don't just write down the first thing that comes into their minds. They think very carefully about which words to use so that they can put over exactly what they want to say. It is the reader's job to try to pick up these clues in order to understand what the writer is trying to say.

We are going to look at a complete story now to see how the narrative genre works and to learn how to unlock this kind of text.

As you read the text for the first time keep in mind two basic questions:

1 What happens in the story?

2 Who is the story about?

Later, we will also ask you some harder questions but these two will be enough to keep in mind for a first reading.

This story was written in the 1970s by a school pupil.

Sparrow

The dim Glasgow morning air closed coldly around the boy as he shuffled along. He pulled his jacket around him in a gesture of defiance. It had been his brother's jacket and was now far too small for him. He tried to pull the sleeves down but every time he let go they crept back up his arms to reveal his white, boney wrists. His breath billowed outwards and upwards to disappear into the towering gaps between the tenements. The faintly tangerine sky scraped through the lofty black gaps above Tommy's head as he scuffled along, lost to the sights and sounds and smells of a desolated Glasgow morning.

His foot kicked out at a lonely stone on the pavement. It rose a few inches and trundled out of sight into a matt black doorway. As he followed it into the darkness, his eye caught a small object huddled into the step.

The sparrow was cold in his hand – almost too cold, but Tommy knew it would live – it was only a matter of time till it lifted its tiny brown head and opened its tiny eyelids. Tommy wandered along, happy in the thought that he had something to fondle on his way to school. The bell rang, and as he was being pushed and jostled someone blasted in his ear:

'Whit ye goat there Tommy?'
'Aw it's jist a sparrow.'
'Where did ye fund it? In a bucket?'
'Naw, in a door doon Margaret's street.'
'Let's see it then.'
'Naw ye'll hurt it.'
'Ah'll no, gies a look.'
'Awright. Bit just a wee yin.'
'Goad, the thing's deid as a doornail ya mug.'
'It's no deid at aw. It's jist sleepin.'

Tommy's heart took a sudden thumping tumble. Perhaps it was dead after all.

'Naw it's no deid it's just sleepin.' He reassured himself and his friend. The classroom was warm and musty and Tommy took up his usual position at the back of the class beside the radiator. Still the sparrow lay. Cold and numb.

He laid his schoolbag under the comforting heat, bunched it up and placed the sparrow on top of it to warm up and live.

'It'll be warm there,' he said to his friend from the lines.
'Ye're daft puttin' it there. Auld Henderson'll see it an' chuck it in the bucket.'

Tommy shrugged off his friend's apprehension.

'Aw, Henderson's blind. He'll never see my sparrow.'

Mr Henderson stormed in – a blustering bully of a man who ruled by the lash, and to whom childhood was merely an unfortunate interlude between birth and adulthood.

'Class stand!' he bellowed. 'Hands together. Our Father, which art in . . .'

Ah wonder whit ah'll call it, thought Tommy, maybe Albert efter ma deid goldfish. Ah could keep it in the auld budgie cage in the attic, till it gets better and . . .

'Amen. Class sit. Sit down Aitken!'
'Sorry sir?' replied Aitken.
'In a dream again, Aitken?'
'No sir.'
'What was it this time Aitken, girls? Eh?' The class giggled.
'No sir.'
'No sir what?'
'No sir. Mr Henderson.'
'That's it Aitken. Sit down boy.'

Tommy flamed inside and longed to launch himself at the man making a fool of him and kick him like the cowboys on the television. Tommy gazed down at the little bird lying limp on his sports bag beside the radiator, its feathers clammy and matted.

And it lay still.

Henderson walked slowly up the passage peering at grubby jotters. Tommy opened his at the next clean page and wondered if Henderson would see the young bird lying by his side.

'Let's see the book then young Aitken. Look at it. Filthy. What on earth is that on top of your bag?'
'A bird, sir.'
'A bird, a bird. Get it out of here. Get it out!'

Before Tommy could move, Henderson had the bird between his fingers and had dropped it deliberately and slowly into the wastepaper bin on the floor.

Tears jerked themselves into the young boy's eyes. His head filled with every abusive term he could think of but he remained silent and hateful. Henderson looked at the boy and smiled.

Tommy was running. Running fast. Over roads without looking. Not hearing the piercing hoot of a car horn as it swerved to avoid him. All he could sense was the sparrow cold in his warm hand. As he struggled breathlessly to the top of the stairway, he could hear his mother calling to him, far off. He laid the young bird beside the crackling fire to warm it and bring it back to life.

'Tommy do you hear me callin'? Ye're early hame. What's that ye're hidin'?'

'Nothin' mum.'

'What's that, a bird? Get it oot ma hoose, ah've jist cleaned the fireplace.'

'Ahm jist warmin' it up mum.'

'Get it oot, can ye no' see that it's deid?'

'It's sleepin mum. Sleepin.'

Without a word or a warning gesture she had scooped the sparrow up in the fireside shovel and dropped it into the fire.

'Muuuuuuum.' He choked on the word. He screamed, the rage tearing at his heart like a tiger caged. He hated her and everybody and he spat his hate out in every swear word he knew as it sprang from his mouth. His mother stood back as each word buried itself home. His fists pounded on her and the screams deafened her. Tommy kicked and screamed his way from the living room to the sanctuary of his bedroom. There in the stillness and silence his thoughts turned to the bird burning in the fire.

His sparrow was dead.

By Benny Placido

Task 1: the gist

The first step in unlocking the text is to work out roughly the answers to the two questions we gave you at the beginning of this section. We've repeated them below to remind you.

1 What happens in the story?

2 Who is the story about?

Work in pairs and talk about the two questions. You don't need to write anything down. Just talk about them and be prepared to tell the rest of the class what you think.

Now you have completed the first step in unlocking the text. You might think that you have worked it all out and there is very little else to be said. We think you are wrong and we hope to show you all the other things that you can unlock.

Task 2: the details

Plot

Again work with a partner to answer this third question.

3 What *exactly* happens in the story?
You need to work out, *in detail*, what happens in the story. Remember that the author put it together very carefully. In a short story, a writer doesn't have time or space to spend on things which don't matter. Nothing happens without a reason.

page 156

Glossary

Layout
The way a text or part of a text is set out or arranged on the page or screen.

Summarise
To pick out and describe briefly in your own words the main points of a text.

Confrontation
Where two characters conflict or disagree with each other.

Draw a timeline of the events in the story. Stick to the main events. We have started a timeline in the style of a mind map to help you, but you might want to lay it out differently. Don't spend too long deciding on your layout. The idea is to summarise the events quickly.

Another hint to get you started is that we think there are *three* main confrontations in the story. What do you think they are? You have 5 minutes, and no more, for this challenge.

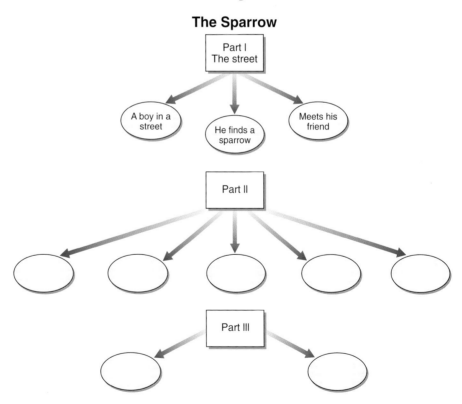

You might have decided that not a lot actually happens in the story. But we still thought it was a good story because it made us think about times when we had lost something which meant a lot to us. So, how did the author make us care about what happens?

He made us care about the character. We are going to look at this aspect of the story next.

5 Unlocking your imagination: characters

The second question we asked you to think about when reading *The Sparrow* was:

● Who is the story about?

Make a list of all of the characters in the story.

Do this now.

Put a number 1 next to the name of the character you think is most important. Number the other characters, right down to a number 4 for the character who is least important.

We think that **Mr Henderson** is quite important and we are going to show you how we unlocked information about him from the text. Then we are going to help you to do the same for Tommy.

We used a *copy* of the story and a coloured highlighting pen.

When we learned something that we thought might be important about Mr Henderson, we highlighted it.

This is our copy of the passage. Would you have highlighted anything different?

Mr Henderson stormed in – a blustering bully of a man who ruled by the lash*, and to whom childhood was merely an unfortunate interlude between birth and adulthood.

'Class stand!' he bellowed. 'Hands together, Our Father, Which art in . . .'

Ah wonder whit ah'll call it, thought Tommy, maybe Albert efter ma deid goldfish. Ah could keep it in the auld budgie cage in the attic, till it gets better and . . .

'Amen. Class sit. Sit down Aitken!'

'Sorry sir,' replied Aitken.

'In a dream again, Aitken?'

'No sir.'

'What was it this time Aitken, girls? Eh?' The class giggled.

'No sir.'

'No sir what?'

'No sir. Mr Henderson.'

'That's it Aitken. Sit down boy.'

*This story was set in the time when pupils used to be hit or 'belted' with a leather belt as a punishment in school.

Once we had highlighted everything that we thought might be important, we went back to the words and phrases we had identified and tried to work out what we thought the author was telling us about Mr Henderson. It helped us to make a table of our notes.

Highlight	What we think it means
Mr Henderson stormed in	He liked to make an entrance. He liked to draw attention to himself. He made a lot of noise and confusion as he came in.
blustering bully	He made a lot of noise but it didn't always make sense. He liked to dominate people and make them frightened of him.
who ruled by the lash	He belted pupils to get them to behave. 'Lash' sounds really cruel; you can almost hear the noise it would make as it swishes through the air.

Now try to work out the rest of the highlighted words and phrases by yourself.

Copy the table below into your jotter and fill in the right-hand column.

Highlight	What I think it means
childhood was merely an unfortunate interlude between birth and adulthood.	
'In a dream again, Aitken?' 'What was it this time Aitken, girls? Eh?'	
'No sir.' 'No sir what?'	
'That's it Aitken. Sit down boy.'	

1   Have a class discussion about your ideas and brainstorm on the board as many new words as you can to describe Mr Henderson.

2   How do you think Tommy feels about him? How do you know this?

3   How do you think the author wants the reader to feel about Mr Henderson? How do you know this?

Now do the same exercise to analyse the character of Tommy.

1 Highlight any words or phrases which tell you something which you think might be important about Tommy. (Remember to do this on a **copy** of the story and not in the book.)

2 Draw a table with two columns, like ours, and write in your notes what you think the author is telling us about Tommy.

Feelings

Think about the **feelings of the different characters** in the story.

● How do *they feel*?

● How do *you feel about them*?

You could make another table to help you to organise your thoughts on this.

Character	Their feelings	My feelings about them
Tommy		
His friend		
Mr Henderson		
Tommy's mum		
The sparrow		

Characterisation

Authors use various strategies or techniques to make us think and feel in certain ways about their characters and plots. What do you think these techniques are?

We have already introduced you to one of these techniques during our study of Mr Henderson: sometimes the author **describes the appearance of the character**.

Look again at the two opening paragraphs. How do you think the author wants us to feel about Tommy? Think about the way the author describes what he looks like.

Can you spot any other techniques? It would be good if you could find some examples of some different techniques.

Once you have done this, turn over and see what we think. Are there any techniques which you and your class have added which we have missed?

Glossary

Characterisation
How an author helps us to imagine what kind of person the character is, e.g. by describing their appearance, things they do or say, or what others say about them.

We spotted these characterisation techniques:

- Sometimes the author gives his or her character **something to do**. Again look at the two opening paragraphs. What does Tommy actually do? Which words in particular make us feel sorry for him and tell us a little about his character?

- Sometimes the author **makes a comment about the character**. Can you find an example of this?

- Sometimes the author makes **one character say something about another character**. Can you find an example of this?

- Sometimes the author gives the characters **something to say** and **makes them say it in a particular way**. This tells us more about them. Look at the dialogue between Tommy and his friend. It doesn't really take the *action* or *plot* forward, but it does tell us something about the two boys. What does it tell us?

In a class discussion work out what you have managed to unlock about the different characters in the story. Once you have done this, read the story over again. Hopefully you will read more into it than you did the first time you read it.

So far you have unlocked lots of information about **plot** and **character** but there are still some other really important elements in this genre.

Let's see if we can work out what these are.

6 Unlocking your imagination: other story features

Setting

Look again at the opening two paragraphs of *The Sparrow*. Use a different colour of highlighter this time and mark any words which tell us **where the story was set**. By this we mean **where it took place**.

- What words does the author use to describe the **setting**?

- Why do you think he chose these words?

- Which words or phrases do you think the author chose especially to create an **atmosphere**?

- What kind of atmosphere is he trying to create? How do you think he wants us to feel at the beginning of the story?

- How do you think he wants us to feel about Tommy?

> ### Glossary
>
> **Setting**
> The place, and what it is like, where the plot happens in a narrative text.
>
> **Atmosphere**
> A feeling or mood which a place creates in us, e.g. an atmosphere of fear in a horror story.

Openings

We often find out about setting in the **opening** of a short story or novel. Openings are very important. They often give us vital information about what to expect later in the story

In a whole class discussion decide why setting is important in telling a story.

Endings

- What do you think of the **ending** of *The Sparrow?*

- Is there anything in particular about the way the story ended that you liked or didn't like? In the ending of this story we were left in no doubt that the sparrow was dead. But stories don't always end like this. Can you think of other kinds of endings?

Word choice and detail

Did you notice that the author of our story chose words very carefully to help us to picture the scene and imagine the atmosphere?

Here are some descriptions we particularly liked. We have also tried to say why we liked them.

Description	Why we liked it
The dim Glasgow morning air closed coldly around the boy	It was almost as if the air of Glasgow was trying to attack him and destroy him.
as he shuffled along	'Shuffled' makes you think of tiny steps, as if he is powerless against the cold and misery of his life.
in a gesture of defiance	He is going to stand up for himself. He is a survivor. It, whatever 'it' is, is not going to get him.

Try some of these by yourself. You could either work in pairs, in groups of four or as a whole class.

Description	Why we liked it
His breath billowed outwards and upwards	
towering gaps between the tenements	
The faintly tangerine sky	
lofty black gaps	
he scuffled along	
His foot kicked out at a lonely stone on the pavement.	
It (the stone) trundled out of sight	
someone blasted in his ear	
Can you add any others?	

Glossary

Visualise
To picture the scene in your mind.

The author also used **small details** to help us visualise what was happening. Tommy kicks the stone into a doorway. But look at the words the author chooses: 'The stone rose a few inches and trundled out of sight into a matt, black doorway.' Tommy is holding the small sparrow in his hand and the author mentions 'It was only a matter of time before it lifted its tiny brown head and opened its tiny brown eyelids.' Can you find any other examples of where the author uses small details to make the picture clear?

You already know about **similes** and **metaphors** from ***Turnstones 1***.

The author just cannot find the words to say how Tommy feels when Mr Henderson bullies him. Instead he uses an **image**.

page 149

Explain how he uses an image when he says this:

'Tommy flamed and longed to launch himself at the man making a fool of him.'

or this:

'He screamed, the rage tearing at his heart like a tiger caged.'

Have a class discussion about the images we use to describe our own anger. Here is one to start you off:

'My mum went ballistic when she saw the mess in my room.'

You could make a class collection of 'anger' images.

Theme

You have unlocked lots of ideas from your close reading of *The Sparrow*. But what do you think it was **really** about? We don't mean the events; we mean what the writer was trying to make you think about. To work this out, try to tell your partner what the story was really about in one sentence. This is hard but here are some hints. Stories are often about certain **themes** like love, hatred, revenge, greed, loss, learning something about yourself, ambition, anger or fear.

Take *Goldilocks and the Three Bears* as an example. The plot is about a girl who goes into a house when the bears are out. She eats their food; breaks their furniture and sleeps in their beds. These are the events, but what do you think the themes are? What was the author really trying to say? Maybe it is about respecting other people's property. Could it be about anything else?

You might want to think about other well known stories and then try to sum up what the author was really on about. But, if you have got the idea, what do you think *The Sparrow* is really about? What are the **themes** in it?

What are the features of a story?

You have done a great deal of work on *The Sparrow* and, on the way, you have learned a lot about the features of the story-telling genre.

Work with a partner to see if you can make a list or a mind map of the most important features that a story must have. We have started a diagram to set you off. Compare your thoughts with another pair before

---

Glossary

Simile
Figurative language where one thing is said to be like or as another, e.g. 'rage tearing at his heart like a tiger caged'.

Metaphor
When one thing is said to be another to help us imagine what is being described, e.g. Tommy 'flamed'; his rage is seen as a sudden eruption of fire.

Image
Usually a picture, such as a photograph; or a group of words which make a picture in our imaginations.

Theme
A main matter which is the central concern of the text, e.g. love, hatred, jealousy, growing up, growing old etc.

having a whole class discussion. Finally, you could make a poster for the wall which sums up all the features you have identified. You will be able to refer to it the next time you have to write in the story genre.

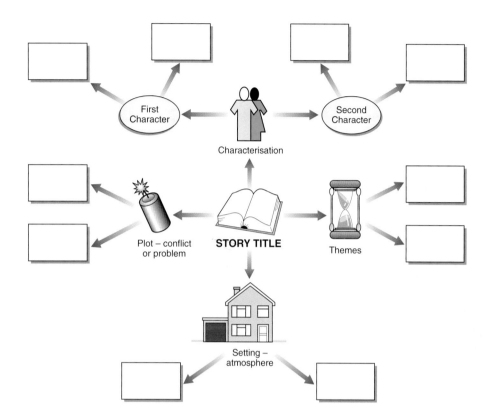

Writing challenge

Now try to write a story of your own. It might be that you too have lost something or someone who meant a great deal to you. Keep your story simple with only a few characters. Give them a problem to solve or a conflict to resolve. Use description, actions and dialogue to show what your characters are like and how they feel. Your **audience** is other people like you and the **purpose** of your writing is to entertain the reader and to help them know how you felt.

Here are some ideas for stories you might tell.

- Do you have a scar? How did you get it?

- What is your earliest childhood memory?

- Has something really sad, funny or embarrassing happened to you?

- Have you lost something or someone that meant a lot to you?

- Have you been lost or found yourself in a strange and unfamiliar place which frightened you?

Before you begin to write, you could think about something which has *really* happened to you. But you can make bits up to make it a better story. Remember, your purpose is to *entertain* your reader or listener, not to tell the truth, the whole truth and nothing but the truth! Try to make your story as interesting as you can by:

- using the best words possible

- putting in lots of details

- including your feelings at different stages.

First of all **tell your story to your partner.** You should take no more than three minutes to do this. Now your partner will tell you his or her story. Again you have only three minutes to do this. Now take another three minutes to discuss how you could make your stories more interesting. Are there any details in your partner's story that you would like to hear more about? Did he or she include descriptions of feelings?

Now group into four. You have had one practice at telling your story. Now tell it again and really go for it! Remember what you are trying to do: entertain your audience by making them laugh, feel sad or feel sorry for the main character.

You should now have lots of ideas for **writing** your story. Use some of the techniques that you learned by analysing *The Sparrow* to write your story, or think about another favourite story to use as a model.

Remember

- **Audience**: Who am I writing for?

- **Purpose**: What am I trying to do with my writing?

- **Features of the short story genre**: What features shall I use?

7 Unlocking your imagination: Scots voices

Glossary

Scots
A language spoken in Scotland and Northern Ireland, descended mainly from the Northumbrian variety of Old English with its influences including Old Norse and Norman French. See also definition for dialect.

Dialect
(Also called a variety.) A language obviously different from related languages in its accent or words and their use, e.g. Doric is the dialect of Scots spoken in Aberdeenshire.

Monologue
One person speaking, usually to an audience in a narrative, play or poem.

Mood
The atmosphere created by a text, e.g. happy, scary, sad etc.

Tone
The feeling or mood expressed by the speaker or writer of a text.

Rhythm
Sound patterns made by a regular emphasising of words or syllables, or by adopting particular sentence structures, e.g. 'Know what I mean?' or 'Not a soul.'

Monologue

In this section we are going to *listen* to a variety of characters talking to us in **Scots** of different **dialects**. So you will need sharp ears. You will also need sharp eyes to catch us when *we* switch to talking in Scots.

We start with voices in **monologue**. A monologue is when one person is speaking aloud, to him or herself or to another person. This can be an effective way to tell a story or to give a snapshot of a person's feelings and thoughts about an event.

Monologues are found in plays, stories and poetry.

Thinking about monologues

A monologue has to *sound right* when spoken out loud and it has to reveal to us a particular character and **mood**. The **voice** has to be right. The voice is made up of a combination of word-choice, **tone** and **rhythm**. The words have to be the words that the particular character would use.

Look at some short extracts from a few monologues. Read them aloud to your partner and see if you can find the right voice for the character.

As you listen, try to work out in:

- **extract 1** – the speaker's *main* complaint, from all the other complaints

- **extract 2** – the problems with special days at this Stonehaven school

- **extract 3** – how the speaker feels about being adopted

- **extract 4** – what the speaker is in two minds about

Monologue 1

Sometimes you feel cut off. Know what I mean? I mean we've been here seven year and I hardly know anybody to talk to. Not a soul. You go outside the door and there's nothing. No wee shops or that. So you walk down the underpass there. Through the tunnel and up the other side. And you wait for a bus to take you to the shopping centre. And there's no glass left in the shelter, so it's freezing. And unless you time it just right you're stuck there for half an hour. So what can you do? And when you get there there's always a kind of empty feeling about it. Even when it's jampacked with folk.

From **Space Invaders** by Alan Spence (Hodder & Stoughton, 1994)

Monologue 2

School sports, 1974, a wee dreich day wi the haar an a' ready, in fae the harbour tae hing aboot the playing fields and turn your knees purple wi' damp and cauld cause yon stupit Ma Hockey reckons we actually get a summer in Stoney*. Telling you, you couldnae see wan hale race, jist fitever bit was closest tae you. Lethal, javelins and shotputs flyin oot o the fog, Tavvy Nichols putted his shot intae the stovie bucket, naebody noticed, that wis school mashed tatties for you. Aye, and that was school catering for you, if it wis the Christmas dance, the concert or the sports it wis aye the same, stovies on a wee paper plate, irn brew or cauld pale broon coffee, that's fit they cried a celebration.

* Stoney is Stonehaven, on the east coast of Scotland.

**From 'Saturday at the Commodore' by Rona Munro, in Scot Free
(Nick Hern Books, 1990)**

Monologue 3

Ma mammy bot me oot a shop
Ma mammy says I was a luvly baby
Ma mammy picked me (I wiz the best)
your mammy had to take you (she's no choice)

From The Adoption Papers by Jackie Kay (Bloodaxe Books Ltd, 1991)

Monologue 4

... Seturday efternune an yince again we're traillin roon the shops luikin fur claes an stuff fur yon bairn ...
... that's aw they dae noo ...
... bet they didnae dae that fur me ...
... A think they've forgotten they hae a dochter ...
... A'm fair forfochen but A juist get STOP YER GIRNIN CATHY IT'S AW YE SEEM TAE DAE NOO WHIT'S WRANG WI YE YE'RE GETTING TAE BE A BIG LASSIE NOO ...
... it's plain tae me that THEY dinnae ken whit's wrang wi me ...
... A mean fair enough a new bairn seems like a guid idea ...
... ken it wuid be a bit like a new doll ...
... A like dollies ...
... but whit if it wis a wee laddie ...

... A dinnae ken if A like wee laddies ...

... Gemma's got a wee brither an aw he dis is mak a richt mess an A mind yince he ripped her new dress ...

... A think A'd like a wee lassie cause A cuid dress her up in bonnie claes ...

... aw frilly fancy an that ...

... juist like a doll ...

... A like dollies ...

... ay but whit if the bairn kep greetin aw the time ...

... A wuidnae like that ...

... an see if it wisnae yin o thae greetin-faced bairns an it wis aw happy an bricht then awbodie wuid love the new bairn mair than me ...

... mind A dinnae think oniebodie loves me the noo oniwey ...

... it's juist like A'm no here an if this is whit it's like the noo whit like'll it be efter thon bairn comes oot ...

... och it cannae be that bad ...

... at least A'll no get the blame fur awthing the wey A dae noo an when it gets aulder an nane o ma pals wants tae play wi me then the bairn'll ayeweys be there an it'll be someyin tae batter when A get bored ...

... Noo whit's it tae be cried ...

... whit aboot Maggie ...

... naw A mind ma great auntie Maggie ...

... A'm shair she wis a witch ...

... whit aboot Gemma like ma pal ...

... naw she's think A'd juist copied her like ...

... A quite like Suzi ...

... ma doll's cried Suzi ...

The Bairn by Andrea Walker

Unlockin the text

Work tae dae

- Talk wi yer teacher aboot yer answers tae the questions we gied ye fur *listenin* tae the monologues.

- Noo *read* the monologues fur yersel. Think aboot the voice ye hear in each monologue. Mind that the voice is a combination o word choice,

Glossary

Appropriate
Suited to; in line with; what you would expect in this genre of text.

Screivin
Scots for 'writing', can be a noun or verb.

Accent
A distinctive way of pronouncing words, often associated with a region, a country or part of a country, e.g. American accent, Aberdonian accent.

tone and rhythm. Answer the followin questions an gie evidence frae the monologue tae back up yer answer.

1 Wha's speakin? When dae we stert tae get ideas aboot the speaker's age and sex?

2 Whit's the speaker talkin aboot? Explain the situation in a couple o sentences.

3 Can ye tell whaur the monologue is takin place?

4 Dae ye think the speaker is talkin tae somebody else or jist tae his or hersel?

5 Whit kin a mood is the speaker in?

6 Is the language **appropriate** tae the character that is speakin?

Writin yer ain monologue in Scots

A monologue is a guid wey tae stert **screivin** in Scots.

Ye wull hae noticed that some Scots voices hae vera little Scots words left in the dialect, though the **accent** may still be vera Scottish. So *you* dinnae hae tae worry hoo much Scots ye ken or yaise.

Here's a wheen scenarios tae choose frae:

● You are a pupil who has to sit through a long, boring school assembly. The Head Teacher is telling the First Years about wearing uniform, being on time and working hard. Write the monologue which is going on in the pupil's head. It can include his or her thoughts on what is being said or on what he or she sees, looking round the room. Perhaps the pupil's thoughts wander to other matters which have nothing to do with what is going on at the assembly.

● You are a 12-year-old boy or girl who has just had a big fight with his or her mum and dad. They received your school report and were not pleased with the comments. You have been sent to your room. Write a monologue outlining your thoughts and feelings about what has happened, perhaps how unfair you think it is or admitting that the comments were true, maybe worrying about what is going to happen to you now.

● Take a story that you know well. Maybe a fairy story like Cinderella or a story you have read in class. Choose one of the characters and write a monologue from his or her point of view. The character does not have to be at the very centre of the story. For example, if you chose Cinderella you could write a monologue as one of the ugly sisters, complaining about Cinderella's good fortune.

HELP! I can't get started . . .

If you're finding it hard to get started, you could use one of these beginnings:

- If he goes on any longer I'm going to fall asleep. School uniform! Again! Nearly everybody's wearing it, anyway. The hall's full of folk in blue sweatshirts. And late coming. Half the time it's the bus that's late.

- Grounded. For two whole weeks. Ah'll go aff ma heid, stuck here lookin at four walls. Ah mean the report wasny that bad. No really. Ah got Excellent in Art. And Good in Science – at least it looks like 'Good'. That Mr Henderson's handwritin's worse than mines.

- Ah dinnae believe it. Naw, cannae be. Prince Chairmin wants tae mairry hur? Whit in the wee man dis he see in hur?

8 Unlocking your imagination: Scots voices

Dialogue

Glossary

Dialogue
Two or more people speaking to each other, usually in a play, but sometimes in a narrative or poem.

A **monologue** is when we hae juist the yin person speakin. **Dialogue** is when we hae mair than yin. So we hae dialogue in novels, short stories, plays an sometimes in poems. The author disnae need juist the yin voice; he needs at least twa.

As we read, we are askin oorsels questions aboot the situation an place but, maist important, aboot the speakers ... the same sort o questions we asked aboot monologue but noo there's mair than yin speaker tae think aboot.

This story by a writer aboot yer ain age is maistly dialogue wi jist a line or twa o narrative, the bits no in inverted commas. Maist o the time she disnae tell us wha's speakin but we ken by the voice.

Listen first tae yer teacher readin the story. Try tae work oot answers tae these questions:

1 Wha are the speakers, and wha is the narrator (i.e. the story-teller)?

2 Whit has happened in the past?

3 Whit is happenin noo?

MAMMIE by LYN HASTON

'Ay, yer Mammie wis a wunnerfu wumman, son.'

'How wis she wunnerfu, Nana? Whit did she look like? Whit did she dae?'

'Ma Goad, fower year auld an aw thae questions!'

'C'moan, Nana.'

'Och, she wis richt bonnie, yer mammie. A richt bonnie wee face she had an a laugh like an angel fae heaven. Her hair wis richt curly when she wis wee, like, an A used tae pit it back in wee pink ribbons fur her.'

'No *pink*, Nana!'

'Ay, son, pink wis her best colour.'

'Did she like trees, Nana? Did she climb trees?'

'Heavens above, no! A proper wee madam she wis an oh ma Goad whit a bonnie dancer! A had her oot every Seturday at clesses an A wis aye makkin costumes fur her. It cost me an yer Granpa a fortune but it wis wurth it juist tae see the smile on her wee face. Wait a bit so, A've got something tae shaw ye.'

She heaved hersel up an gaed ben tae the bedroom, wipin a tear fae her ee as she gaed.

Ben she cam again wi a wee wuiden box.

'Tak a wee look at this, son,' she said haunin it me. 'A want ye tae hae them when ye're big.'

A tuik a keek inside an A cuidnae believe ma een. Hunners o beautifu medals, gowden an siller!

'Aw thaim wis fae her dancin,' ma Nana smiled proodly. Her een kinna glazed owre an she wis awa in her ain wurld, lookin roond at the photies o ma Granda an ma uncles. Her pale wrinkled face wis lost in shaddies but A cuid see by the licht in the corner monie a tear glistenin doon her cheek. A wis only fower an A didnae ken whit tae say tae a wumman that distressed.

'Dinnae greet, Nan,' A begged. 'Ye've still got me!'

She took me tae her an hugged me ower ticht fur ma likin but A didnae say naething. 'That's richt, wee laddie. An ye're aw that maitters. But whit'll ye dae when A'm gane, wee man?' she speirt.

'Och, Nana, dinnae fash yersel, A'll be fair grown up then.'

'Ay, that ye will, an yer parents wuid be prood o ye.'

'Ma parents? A didnae ken A had a Da, Nana. Whit wis he like?'

'Goad, laddie, enough questions! Get yersel tae yer bed.'

'Och, Nana.'

'Awa ye gae!'

'Will ye tell us te morn, Nana?'

'Mebbe.'

'Will ye?'

'Get tae yer bed.'

'Richt, Nana.'

A gaed ben tae ma room, next tae the wee kitchen, got intae ma bed an gaed tae sleep . . .

As a group or whole class, discuss the questions set at the beginnin o the extract.

Wi a pairtner, try readin the story wi yin o ye readin the grannie's pairt an the ither the wee laddie's. Then see if the pair o ye kin jalouse the answers tae the questions.

1 Frae the first bit o the dialogue, hoo much dae we learn aboot whit happened tae the bairn?

2 Hoo dae the narrative bits (a) move the story furrit? (b) mak us feel sorry fur the Nana?

3 Hoo dae we jalouse wha's speakin (a) frae whit they say? (B) frae the wey they say it?

4 The twa speakers baith speak Scots but the writer has gien each their ain voice. Usin quotations, show hoo.

5 Whit dae ye think is the story o the wee laddie's parents – are they deid, separatit or whit? Will the grannie tell the laddie aboot his faither the morn? If so, whit will her story be. Tell it yersel, wi the laddie interruptin tae speir questions at her, but **dinnae write it doon**. Discuss whit the story micht be, then **improvise**. Juist mind that ye hae tae try an speak in character. Yaise the voice o the grannie an the wee laddie. When ye've gaed through it twa or three times, dae it in front o anither pair or the hail class.

Screivin in Scots

Noo, try screivin yer ain dialogue in Scots. It cuid be a script, a short story, an extract fae a novel, or even a poem but it has tae be maistly speech, twa folk speakin tae yin anither. Ye'll mebbe no even hae tae say wha's speakin, if the voices are clearly different the reader will ken, but mind a new paragraph every time.

Ye'll need twa different folk wi twa different voices –

- yin auld, the ither young?
- yin male, the ither female?
- yin human, the ither no (an animal, an alien)?
- yin Scots, the ither English?

1 Whit is it they're talkin aboot?

2 Where are they?

3 Whit is the main thing ye're tryin tae dae? Tell a story? Show whit the characters are like? Or a bit o baith? Whitever, ye hae tae dae it through the dialogue wi as little narrative as possible.

9 Fun challenge: found poems

A found poem is made up of words and phrases taken from something you have read or heard. It uses someone else's words but you combine them in a different way which is special to you. You have to think very carefully what the person who wrote or spoke the original meant. Then you have to find the best words or phrases that *they* use which really help *you* to picture the meaning of the text. Then you lay them out in a different way so that you put a new meaning or 'spin' on the words and you find a new poem which is yours. This is actually much easier to do than to describe.

Read the passage below or your teacher may read it to you. Think about some of these questions:

- What is the writer trying to do with his writing?

- How is he trying to make you feel?

- What is he trying to make you think of?

Discuss the questions with the class or with a partner.

You will be given a copy of the passage. Read it again and, by yourself, underline the words and phrases you particularly like. We have done one or two for you to give you the idea. Afterwards you will have to explain why you chose those words. Your teacher might organise a paired or group discussion for you to share your ideas.

The listeners

When I looked up, the trees had <u>closed in above my head like a prison roof</u> and I couldn't see the smallest patch of sky or a single star. I couldn't see anything at all. <u>The darkness was so solid around me I could almost touch it.</u>

'Dad!' I called out. 'Dad, are you there?'

My small high voice echoed through the forest and faded away. I listened for an answer, but none came.

I cannot possibly describe to you what it felt like to be standing alone in the pitchy blackness of that silent wood in the small hours of the night. The sense of loneliness was overwhelming, the silence was as deep as death, and the only sounds were the ones I made myself. I tried to keep absolutely still for as long as possible to see if I could hear anything at all. I listened and listened. I held my breath and listened again. I had a queer feeling that the whole wood was listening with me, the trees and the bushes, the little animals hiding in the undergrowth and the birds nesting in the branches. All were listening. Even the silence was listening. Silence was listening to silence.

I switched on the torch. A brilliant beam of light reached out ahead of me like a long white arm. That was better. Now at any rate I could see where I was going.

From Danny the Champion of the World by Roald Dahl (Jonathan Cope, 1975)

Finding your poem

Look carefully at the words you have chosen and lay them out on the page so that they look like a poem. You can change some of the words or add others. It's up to you.

Challenges

- How can you draw attention to some very important words?

- How will you punctuate your poem to help the reader understand your meaning?

This is how a pupil called John started his poem:

I'm alone!
Forest trees had closed in above my head
Like a prison roof.
I couldn't see the smallest patch of sky.
The dark was like a brick wall.

Once you have tried this out for yourself, look at the rest of John's found poem. Is yours as good as this?

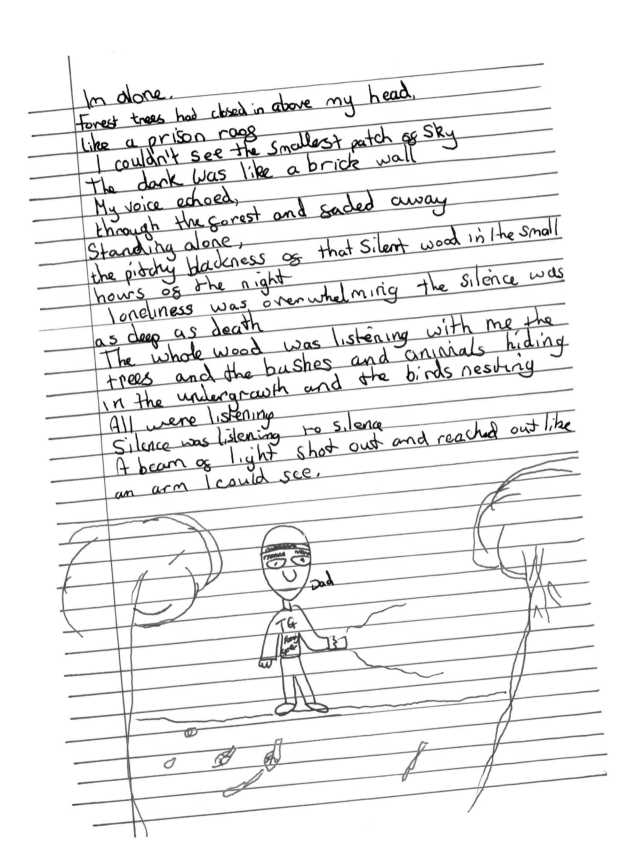

I'm alone.
Forest trees had closed in above my head,
Like a prison roof
I couldn't see the smallest patch of sky
The dark was like a brick wall
My voice echoed,
through the forest and faded away
Standing alone,
the pitchy blackness of that silent wood in the small
hours of the night
loneliness was overwhelming the silence was
as deep as death
The whole wood was listening with me the
trees and the bushes and animals hiding
in the undergrowth and the birds nesting
All were listening
Silence was listening to silence
A beam of light shot out and reached out like
an arm I could see.

Dad
TG

Below we have typed out John's poem and we have made a few changes.
What do you think we did and why do you think we made these changes?
Which version do you prefer?
Why?

I'm alone!

Forest trees had closed in above my head
Like a prison roof.
I couldn't see the smallest patch of sky.
The dark was like a brick wall.
My voice echoed
Through the forest
... and faded away.
Standing alone,
The pitchy blackness of that silent wood in the small hours of the
night.
Loneliness was overwhelming. The silence was as deep as death.
The whole wood was listening with me.
The trees and the bushes and the animals hiding in the undergrowth
and the birds nesting.
All were listening.
To me.
Silence was listening to silence.
A beam of light reached out like an arm.
My torch.
I could see!

You might want to go back to your own poem and make a few changes to:

- the words you have chosen

- the way you have punctuated it

page 156

- the way you have laid it out.

War Horse

Here is another passage. Can you find a poem in it too?

Joey is a horse who was taken to France to 'fight' in the First World War.
During the war he had a number of jobs to do: he carried a brave soldier
until the soldier was killed; he pulled an ambulance wagon with many
injured men in it back to safety.

Michael Morpurgo, the author, tries to imagine what it must have felt like to be this horse, alone and afraid in a strange land. He writes the story as if it is Joey who is speaking, telling us about his experiences. The passage is about something he remembers very vividly. He has been separated from another horse, his friend Topthorn ...

War Horse

When I awoke it was dark and the guns were firing once more all around me. No matter where I looked, it seemed the sky was lit with yellow flashes of gunfire and intermittent white, glowing lights that pained my eyes and showered daylight briefly onto the countryside around me. Whichever way I went it seemed it had to be towards the guns. Better I thought to stay where I was. Here at least I had grass in plenty and water to drink. I had made up my mind to do just that when there was an explosion of white light above my head and the rattle of a machine-gun split the night air, the bullets whipping into the ground beside me. I ran again and kept running into the night, stumbling frequently in the ditches and hedges until the fields lost their grass and the trees were mere stumps against the flashing skyline. Wherever I went now there were great craters in the ground filled with murky stagnant water.

It was as I staggered out of one such crater that I lumbered into an invisible coil of barbed wire that first snagged and then trapped my foreleg. I felt the barbs tearing into my skin before I broke clear. I must have limped on for miles but where to and where from I shall never know. All the while my leg throbbed with pain and on every side of me the great guns were sounding out and rifle-fire spat into the night. Bleeding, bruised and terrified beyond belief, I longed to be with Topthorn again. He would know which way to go, I told myself. He would know.

From **War Horse** by Michael Morpurgo (Mammoth)

Remember to think about the author's purpose when reading writing like this:

- What is the writer trying to do in this extract?
- How is Joey feeling?
- How does Michael Morpurgo want *you* to feel about Joey?

Now underline the words or phrases you think are effective.

Think about how you can lay them out as a found poem to draw attention to certain parts.

Do you want to add any words of your own? You can change the meaning a little but don't change the mood of the original passage.

If you would like to know more about how animals were used in war time, check out this website:

http://www.ku.edu/~kansite/ww_one/photos/greatwr2.htm#animals

You can find out more about Michael Morpurgo and other writers on this website:

http://www.literacytrust.org.uk/campaign/morpugo.html

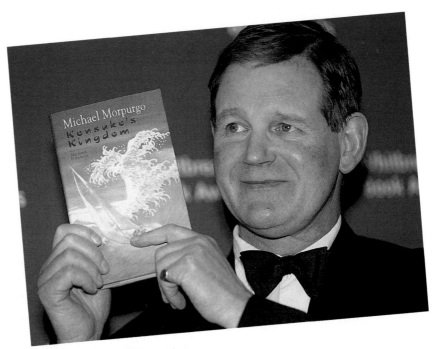

Michael Morpurgo

Finding poems in unusual places

You can find poems in other kinds of writing too. Here is a short piece of text where the writer is giving his views on the Internet. He is trying to persuade the reader that using the Internet is easy if you buy and use his little book.

This time, pick out the words and phrases that you think the author thought were important to get his message across. Do you agree with them?

Read me

There's nothing worse than falling behind – when everyone is talking about something, but it just doesn't gel. The Internet's had this effect over the last few years. Everything you pick up. Internet this, cyber that. But, unless you've been connected you're still in the dark. Getting to grips with the Net can be daunting. The truth is you don't need a fat book to get started on the Internet. It's too much work. And boring. This Rough Guide gives it to you straight. In plain English. We think the Net is a pushover. If you can figure out how to use a word processor, you'll master the Internet.
WELL WHAT ARE YOU WAITING FOR?

From **The Internet: The Rough Guide 1999** by Angus Kennedy (Penguin, 1999)

Again think about how you can lay the words out for the most impact.

You can find poems everywhere you look, even in your homework for another subject! Try finding a poem in history or science.

We have been looking at fairly depressing extracts so far. Here is a slightly more up-beat one for you to puzzle over. It is written as if we are inside the head of another animal. What kind of animal do you think it is? You will need to find evidence for your answer.

Discuss with your partner who – or what – you think Shade is. What clues does the author give you?

Skimming over the banks of the stream, Shade heard the beetle warming up its wings. He flapped harder, picking up speed as he homed in on the musical whine. He was almost invisible against the night sky, the streaks of silver in his thick black fur flashing in the moon's glow.

Airborne now, the beetle was a whirl of shell and wing. Shade still couldn't see it with his eyes – but he could see it with his ears. Caught in his echo vision, the insect hummed and glowed in his mind like a shadow edged with quicksilver. The air whistled in his flared ears as he swooped down. Braking sharply, he scooped the beetle up with his tail membrane, flicked it into his left wing, and volleyed it straight into his open mouth. He veered up and away, and cracked the hard shell with his teeth, savouring the delicious beetle meat as it squirted down his throat. After a few good chomps, he swallowed it whole. Very tasty!

Beetles were far and away the best food in the forest. Mealworms and midges weren't bad either. Mosquitoes didn't taste like much – gauzy, a little prickly at times – but they were the easiest to catch. He'd already eaten over six hundred this evening, something like that anyway, he'd lost count. They were so slow and clumsy all you had to do was keep your mouth open and swallow every once and a while.

His ears pricked up suddenly. It was the tell tale drumming of a tiger moth in flight. He tilted his right wing and wheeled, locking onto his prey. If he could catch one – everyone knew how hard they were to catch – and then he'd have a story of his own to tell back at Tree Haven at sunrise

From Silverwing by Kenneth Oppel, Hodder & Stoughton, 1999

Now read the extract again. It is the opening of a story by Kenneth Oppel called *Silverwing.* The author decided to tell the story through the eyes of Shade. Why do you think he did this? He also wanted to make us think about who Shade is and to have certain feelings about the character. Think about these things when you are 'finding' your poem.

page 156

You might want to look at the section on layout before you do a final draft of your poem.

10 Unlocking the text: mass media

Glossary

Mass media
Forms of communication that reach large numbers of people through e.g. books, newspapers, radio, television, films, music, the Web.

Did you know that two of the most important photographers in the early years of photography were Scots? David Octavius Hill (born in Perth 1802, died 1870) and Robert Adamson (born in Edinburgh 1821, died 1848) collaborated to produce some of the greatest photographic portraits of the nineteenth century.

Photographs and posters

We all learn mainly by using our eyes to interpret what is happening around us. (Though sometimes when, for example, the toast is burning, we learn through other senses as well!) Our eyes are very smart interpreters of the real world.

But the invention of the camera in the nineteenth century and of the movie-camera in the twentieth century has meant that our eyes now need to be smarter than ever. Because when a photographer or film-maker shows us pictures of what *seems* to be the real world, it isn't the real world at all! No longer are *we* choosing what to look at – we are looking only at what the **photographer or film-maker** wants us to see. And the truth is, we can't trust them an inch.

They are up to all sorts of tricks. And the best way to make sure that your eyes can still outsmart them is to *learn* their tricks – to unlock photographs and posters.

Photography tricks

Types of photographs

Here are eight different types of photograph:

- **A** News
- **B** Portrait
- **C** Family
- **D** Sports
- **E** Advertising
- **F** Movie still
- **G** Popular music
- **H** Social.

Task 1

With a partner, can you match the following eight, numbered photographs to these eight, lettered types?

Now, that was easy, wasn't it? Here's the difficult bit: WHY was it easy? Talk about this with your partner for no more than 4 minutes, and note your ideas down. Report back to the class.

You should now have realised that there's two ways to think of answers to this question – the easy way and the hard way. The easy way has to do with looking at immediate content – a photograph of a pop group tells you instantly what it's about, doesn't it? But if we look at matters from another **perspective** things become more complicated. You could try to identify all the signs which are normally included in each type of picture. That would allow you to try to break the **code** for each picture.

Task 2

Now, let's scramble the **images**. Let's say that 1 is the **movie still**; 2 the advertising photograph; 4 the portrait; 6 the family shot; 8 the news photograph.

With a partner, decide what the photographs might be being used for now. In what ways do we look at them differently now? Take no more than 10 minutes to do this. Write your views down, then compare notes with another pair.

Talk about the tasks in class. Discuss, in particular, the idea of the **context** – where the photograph appears; how it has been made; what you are seeing that is *not* the obvious content – and how this context changes your interpretation of the image.

You can see examples of this trick (using the context to change the meaning) in television advertisements every night. Note them down and talk about them to the class.

Glossary

Perspective
Viewpoint or point of view. 'Another perspective' means to look at something in a quite different way.

Code
The features of something (like a type of photograph) which, once recognised, allow you to identify it.

Images
Usually a picture, such as a photograph; or a group of words which make a picture in our imaginations.

Movie still
A single frame from a film, turned into a photograph.

Context
All the aspects of a situation which are affecting the event being discussed.

Film posters

1 Information about film posters

Film posters, or – to use the more glamorous American name – movie posters have been around for a long time now. They are taken for granted by most of us, but some film fans consider them to be collectors' items.

There are several different kinds:

- sheet posters
- lobby card posters
- title cards
- Australian daybill posters
- international posters
- advance posters
- video posters.

Glossary

Copy
Used as a noun, it refers to text written for publication, e.g. by a newspaper or for a poster.

Trailer
An extract from a film or TV show, shown in advance and designed to whet your appetite.

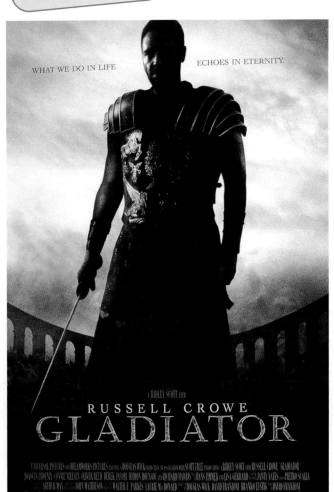

For the purpose of this task, we are interested in the workings of one type of film poster – the **advance** (or 'teaser') poster. This might be related to the actual film release, or to the subsequent video and DVD versions.

An advance poster is intended for use *before* a film's release and is usually similar to a 'normal' poster. It does, however, have additional copy, such as 'Coming this Summer'.

The **teaser** is a special type of advance poster designed to arouse interest, but *not* reveal much information about the film. In a sense, the teaser is similar to certain forms of cinema trailers. All teasers are advance posters, but not all advance posters are teasers!

2 A real film poster (and how it was made)

Here is a real film poster for a film called *Gladiator*. It looks simple but it is really very clever at making us think this might be a film we would want to see. Work in pairs or small groups and think hard about the following questions. If you can answer them, you will know all the tricks you need to make your own poster.

1 In what way is this poster a 'teaser'? How does it intrigue us?

2 What kind of audience is the poster aimed at?

3 What can you actually *see* in the poster? (What you can actually see is called the **denotation** of the poster.)

4 What is *suggested* by the poster about what we will find enjoyable in the film? (What is suggested is called the **connotation** of the poster.)

It is not easy to train your eyes to be as super-smart as this, so here are some extra questions to help you analyse this particular poster.

Analysing the visuals

The main figure shown in the poster is, presumably the 'gladiator' of the title.

1 Does he look like a gladiator should look? Give reasons for your answer.

2 How is he 'placed' in relation to everything around him? What conclusions can we draw from this 'placement'?

3 How would you describe the way he is standing?

4 Why is his sword drawn?

5 What kind of expression does he have? Why is it this kind of expression?

6 Who are the crowds of people?

7 What is the building? Where is it?

8 Why is there a dominant gold colouring throughout the image?

9 Why is it making use of some form of silhouette?

Analysing the text

We have already seen that the visual contains denotation and connotation. There is also **denotation** and **connotation** in the *words* of the poster. If you want to extend your skills, here are some questions to get you thinking:

1 Denotation – What simple *factual information* is given in the words of the poster?

2 Connotation – What *suggestions* are being put into our minds by the layout, lettering, slogan and quotation in the poster. The questions below will help you analyse the textual connotations.

a) What do you notice about the film title, the principal actor's name, and the director's name?

b) What does this tell you about the relative importance of each of these three elements, as far as advertising the film is concerned?

c) What is suggested by the *way* the lettering is presented in the film's title? (Think about both **style** and **typeface**).

d) What comments can you make about the **slogan** used in the poster?

e) What techniques has the slogan-writer used to 'sell' the film, so that an audience will be interested in going to see it?

f) Is the slogan a line from the film? If so, who says it?

g) What might it suggest about the person who says it?

> These questions are quite hard. We have offered you our suggested answers on pages 57–58. Compare them to see if your ideas are better than ours!

Checking out the history of the film poster and the variations of poster would make an interesting research task! Apart from raiding the school library, you could try websites such as the following:

www.movieposters.com
www.filmposters.com

Glossary

Style
The ways a writer or artist or poster designer expresses him or herself for particular effects.

Typeface
The kind of lettering used in a text.

Slogan
A short phrase or statement designed to catch people's attention and sum up a more complex set of ideas or circumstances.

page 79

Tackling another movie poster

Finding Forrester

You should remember the questions which we asked about the *Gladiator* poster, both in terms of the **visual** and the **text** analysis. To what extent can those questions help you tease out the 'messages' contained in the poster for *Finding Forrester*?

Once you have done this, answer the questions below. We think they may help you see how this poster is different in some respects from the *Gladiator* poster.

Analysing the visuals

- Two men are walking together. Who are they?

  - What is their relationship with each other?

  - What details about each of them can you identify?

  - Why, for example, does one character appear to be pointing to or at something?

- There is a larger image of one of the two characters top right. Why is this so?

  - What does this suggest to you?

  - What does this image of the character suggest to you?

- One of the images offered is a city back-drop. Where is it?

- Is it identifiable in terms of its country?

- What does this tell us about the film's **setting**?

- There is also an image of a tenement building left.

  - Who lives here?

  - Which character?

  - What does the building suggest about the occupant(s)?

- The bicycle? Whose is it?

  - Does it have any significance?

- What about the poster's colouring?

  - What do you notice about the colours?

  - What are they suggesting to us?

Analysing the text

- What about the film's title? Who is Forrester?

  - What does 'Finding' mean? What techniques does the title use?

- The **slogan** used in the poster informs us that: '*In an ordinary place he found the one person to make his life extraordinary.*' What comments can be made about the ideas and language contained in the slogan?

- What significance is there in the fact that the poster highlights Sean Connery's name?

- In addition to this, the poster tells us that this film is: 'From the director of *Good Will Hunting*.' Why is this fact highlighted?

Now it is your turn

Before we reach the end of the chapter, we challenge *you* to be the poster-designer who is trying to create interest in *Nessie the Monster* movie. You can devise your poster in any way you like, but it *has* to use some of the tricks of the trade we have been studying.

Task 3

Here's your scenario: you are commissioned to make a poster for a new Scottish film. It is a monster movie featuring Nessie rising from the loch to avenge itself on yet another expedition that is trying to capture it and, in so doing, is disturbing its habitat.

To help you on your way, we have given you:

1 Information about Nessie (below)

2 Information about film posters

3 A real film poster, and some help in seeing how it has been made

Information about Nessie

The Daily Mail on Wednesday, August 12th 1992, carried a story entitled 'Nessie rears her ugly head again (But don't forget this *is* the Silly Season)'. Under this heading was a colour photograph showing a stretch of the loch at one of its narrowest parts, and a protruding length of neck and a head that shines in the light. A classic Nessie picture, taken by 'a 45-year-old man who wishes to keep his identity secret.'

The man, who had been camping a couple of miles from Fort Augustus, went to the loch to wash his face in the early hours of that morning. Looking up, he blinked. He said, 'There was about six feet of a long neck and head and she was a blackish dark brown. She seemed to be looking right at me and I thought she was going to come to the shore. My camera (a Boots 110EF pocket model) was lying by the tree ... And I made a dive for it.

'I scrambled back. She was about forty yards out, still looking in my direction. I was trembling and my heart was pounding but I managed to knock off four shots.
'At one stage she opened her mouth. I thought she was going to make her breakfast of me.'

After submerging for five minutes, the beast resurfaced, together with four or five humps. The witness said, 'It was as if a miniature waterfall was cascading from the front hump'. Then she swam slowly away from him and submerged.

From **The Loch Ness Monster** by Lynn Picknett (Pitkin Ltd, 1993)

More scenario

Before the expedition set out to find the monster and drag it up out of the loch, Nessie rescues a group of teenagers (much like yourselves). They had set out, without their parents' knowledge, on a midnight fishing expedition on the loch. Nessie's wash overturned their dinghy and they might have drowned.

When, later, Nessie comes seeking revenge on the expedition, what part can the teenagers play?

So, you have a choice of ingredients for your poster:

1 The loch

2 Nessie

3 The expedition – you choose who makes up the expedition team

4 The teenagers

5 The teenagers' parents

6 The people who live round the loch, and the tourists (who might have differing reactions to the sight of an avenging monster)

7 Possibly the emergency services or the army who might be called in when Nessie gets shirty.

Things you have to decide in order to make your photograph or poster

1 What is the story's **genre** going to be: a monster thriller with a violent end or a feel-good story with a happy ending?

2 Who is your audience likely to be: adults wanting to be scared or Disney-minded kids?

3 What *kind* of poster will tease them to come?

4 What *ingredients* will go into the poster (its **denotation**)?

5 How will you arrange these ingredients in order to suggest the kind of film you want it to be (its **connotations**)?

That's all the help you're getting. Now get on with it! Be prepared, when you are finished and your poster is pinned to the wall, to explain your choices and tricks to the class.

Finished very quickly?

Here are two other tasks to keep you occupied:

1 With a partner, assemble a collection of about 20 photographs from newspapers and magazines (ask your mums and dads before you start cutting out) and bring them into class. Sort the photos into six categories, labelled A to F. Trim away any evidence that you used to classify the photos, such as written language – **captions**, advertising etc. Exchange your collection for another. Now, you have to identify, the **genre** and audience for each category, showing how the **codes** of the photograph told you what they were. Meet in a group of four to discuss your findings on the other pair's photo collection.

2 With a partner, assemble a collection of about 20 photographs from newspapers and magazines (ask your mums and dads before you start cutting out) and bring them into class. Pick eight or nine examples. Label them A, B etc. Trim away any written language – **captions**, advertising etc. The task here is to arrange them in an order which tells a story. Exchange your set with another pair. Try to discover the story. Meet with the other pair to discuss the stories, how you identified the **genre** and the **codes** that relate to it.

Possible answers to questions on the *Gladiator* poster

Analysing the visuals

1 He is wearing armour and carrying a sword like gladiators did. But he has no protection for his head and the armour looks more ceremonial than practical.

2 He's big (he's in the **foreground**)! Other things around him look 'small' and so less important.

3 He's strong, powerful and commanding, perhaps a leader?

4 He's a 'fighter'.

5 He's serious, thoughtful, intense. To suggest someone with a weight of responsibility or someone facing great danger.

6 The crowds might be the audience come to see him fight; or they might be people ready to follow his leadership.

7 The building is an arena, like a theatre, perhaps an amphitheatre? Could it be in Rome or in one of the countries under Roman control, where they built amphitheatres?

8   The background suggests a 'sunset' or an 'ending'. The gold colour suggests power and wealth.

9   The silhouette effect suggests trickery, treachery and 'hidden' things.

Analysing the text

a)   'Gladiator' is in bold, gold lettering. The actor's name is in white lettering, but put above the title to give it importance. The director's name is at the top of the text, and is in gold to associate him with the film; but his name is much smaller than the actor's name.

b)   It tells you that the title is likely to be of most value in advertising the film; and the actor is of more value than the director.

c)   It suggests 'character', by the firm, formal typeface and is spread wide across the page.

d)   The slogan suggests by 'we' that the gladiator is like all of us, in that the decisions he makes and the acts he performs will be how he is remembered.

e)   It suggests that our deeds in life are remembered when we die, only if they are big and bold like the gladiator's. This makes us want to see what he was like.

f)   Yes, probably spoken by the gladiator.

g)   The gladiator is someone who knows his actions will make him immortal.

This *Gladiator* poster is actually only one in a short series of posters which accompanied the film. As a further piece of research, you could find the other versions which were used.

11 Unlocking the text: mass media

Film

In the last section you learned about some of the tricks used by photographers and poster-designers. In this section you will learn about the tricks used by film-makers.

Feature films can last from about one and a half hours to four hours. But film-makers plan in short sequences which might take only one minute. Your challenge is to plan a sequence of shots for *Nessie the Monster* movie ... and to carry them out.

What is a sequence?

In the same way as you know the **code** for getting the words in a sentence in the right order (you don't say, for example, 'Name my John is'), the film-maker has codes for conveying his messages. His 'sentence' is a sequence of shots; and to make sense they come in a definite order.

An **aerial or long shot** is taken from above (using a crane or a helicopter) or from the ground. It lets us see the whole environment, perhaps a city, landscape or loch, in which the action will take place.

An **establishing shot** shows one or more of the characters (though we may not see their features) taking up a particular place in the environment.

A **mid shot** takes in the character(s) in more detail, so that we can now see clearly who they are and what they are doing.

A **close-up** shot shows us the detail of a character's face or of an object, like a turning doorhandle. It is good for showing the emotion on a face or for raising suspense.

A **panning or tracking shot** swivels the camera to catch sight of something in the immediate area, perhaps mimicking the character's eye-movement; or just following the character's movement.

Another **mid shot** may now be used to relieve the tension or to start to move the action in a new direction.

Task 1

Now you try it. What happens next in the film strip? Draw a film strip like the one above. Use the same sequence of shot types to create another mini-climax (perhaps Nessie's wash overturning the boat).

Influencing the *audience* (remember *denotation* and *connotation*?)

So where's the trickery we were promised? So far it is just about good story-telling technique. The trickery starts when the film-maker wants you to think or feel about the characters in a certain way.

First, some more technical language

- **Mise en scene** is the way a single shot or short series of shots is planned on the film set. In our short sequence, for example, great care would be taken to get the model of Nessie at just the right distance from the boat. *Mise en scene* is exactly what the director decides to put into the shot(s).

- **Montage** is the finished product – the sequence of shots once it is filmed, edited and ready to be shown.

It is at the *Mise en scene* that all the trickery takes place. Here's how.

Camera angles

Camera angles influence how we feel and think about what we see in a film. Look back at the sequence on the previous page. What attitude would we want a cinema audience to have to the monster? Just interest in what Nessie will do? Sympathy for Nessie? Fear for the teenagers? Well, by using exactly the same sequence of shots but with a *different camera angle*, you can get the reaction you want. Make your own choice from the following options.

1 Camera above the subject and pointing downwards – makes the subject look smaller and less threatening.

2 Camera under subject and pointing upwards – makes subject look unnaturally large and threatening.

3 Camera side-on to subject, at subject height – enables us to look calmly at the subject, to be interested in what turn the action is going to take.

4 Camera close up to subject. This is the most influential of the angles but the effect comes from how we show the subject: is Nessie to be shown with savage teeth or big friendly eyes?

Camera focus

Altering the viewing angle is not all that the film-maker can do with the camera. He or she can also change the **focus** on the camera to get some special effects. And these effects can be used in the same way as camera angles to influence the audience.

1 **Shallow focus** makes the subject stand out sharply, catching your attention. Only the foreground can be seen clearly; background is fuzzy.

2 **Deep focus** lets the audience take in all aspects of the situation. The foreground and background are both clear and we can see, in this case, that Nessie is very close to the boat.

3 **Soft focus** softens the lines of the subject by using special filters or lenses. The subject can look more romantic, sympathetic or sinister.

Looking back now to the original sequence we gave you about the teenagers spotting Nessie, which focus would you use for each shot?

Lighting

In the early days of film-making the only source of light was the sun. Sets were built on rotating motors so that they could be turned to face the sun. Obviously, this meant that filming could only take place during daylight hours. Today, however, controlled lighting plays a huge part in the making of films. Lighting is often used to create particular effects. It can also be used to grab our attention, much as the camera shot and use of focus do.

Some lighting terms

- **Key light:** this is usually the main light that lights the character or scene.

- **Filler light:** Usually positioned at the side, a filler light can soften lines. It has a similar effect to a soft focus lens.

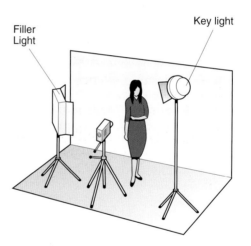

Filler Light

Key light

- **Back light:** the main source of lighting in this case comes from behind the subject being filmed, giving the appearance of a shadow or silhouette.

This subject is lit with a back light.

Whilst lighting is primarily used to allow us to see clearly what is being presented, it can also be used to create effects or particular **atmospheres**. In your groups, discuss for each shot which kind of lighting would go best with the choices you have already made about camera angle and focus.

Sound effects/music

Music is a powerful way of influencing an audience's reactions to your film. Adding slow, sad music can make us cry! Adding fast music can make us even more excited by a high-speed car-chase. Adding a heavy 'heart-beat' rhythm can create suspense.

So think now about what kind of music could be added to the sequence of shots we gave you about the teenagers' first sighting of Nessie by moonlight.

Your turn to be the film-maker

Now go back to Task 1, in which you planned your *own* sequence of shots for the film. Draw and fill out a planning grid like the one given below. Plan your film sequence carefully.

Order of shot	Content of shot (draw or describe)	Type of shot	Position of camera	Camera focus (shallow, deep, etc.)	Lighting	Music
1						
2						
3						
4						
5						
6						

12 Unlocking the text: mass media

Newspapers

In this section you will be working out for yourself the differences between two kinds of newspaper.

To start you off, here are dictionary definitions for the two types.

Tabloids	Broadsheets
Newspapers which give their news in concentrated and easily understood formats.	Newspapers which give a full account of news items in formal language.

That doesn't tell us very much, so let's have a look at the same item of news as it was reported in the two kinds of newspaper.

Extract A

Lottery winner delighted with windfall

James O'Toole, a thirty-year old unemployed labourer from Glasgow who lost his job only three weeks ago, yesterday celebrated a lottery win which provided him with a £3 000 000 windfall. Asked about how he would invest his winnings, he stated that he would take a well-earned holiday, since he had not enjoyed such a luxury for some years. In addition to a holiday, he indicated that he planned to invest some of his money in buying a new house and changing his B-registration Ford Fiesta for a more recent model; Mr O'Toole said he was delighted with his winnings.

Extract B

I'M LOADED SAYS LUCKY LOTTERY WINNER

JIMMY O'TOOLE, A GLASGOW MAN DOWN ON HIS LUCK, YESTERDAY SCOOPED A FANTASTIC £3 MILLION LOTTERY JACKPOT.

The Springburn man, who recently lost his job as a building-worker, nailed the lucky numbers in this week's lottery draw.

Delighted

'Ah cannae believe ma luck', was how the jackpot-winner responded when asked how he felt. 'Pure fantastic, man!' he added.

'This means nae mare problems! A holiday at last an' a chance tae buy a 'real' car. Ah just cannae believe ma luck. The missus'll also be delighted! We can even think aboot buyin' a new hoose wi' this dough!'

Another Glasgow winner

Jimmy is the second lucky Glaswegian punter to claim fabulous lottery megabucks this year, following in the footsteps of Betty Blair last January.

You should be starting to see the differences now. To explore them a bit more, take a full page of your notebook and divide it up as shown below. The column on the left lists the features of newspapers which vary between tabloids and broadsheets. Your challenge is to decide what the differences are. The first feature, Headlines, we have done for you.

	Feature	Tabloid	Broadsheet
Differences in design and layout	Headlines	Catchy, big, bold, dramatic. Uses exclamation and quotation.	Smaller, undramatic. Report is very restrained (e.g. delighted).
	Use of columns/ full-page spread		
	Use of subheadings		
	Use of different fonts		
Differences in story-telling	Amount of factual information		
	Use of quotation/ reported speech		
	Human-interest additions to story		
	Dramatisation of events		
Differences in language	Use of formal/informal language		
	Formal/informal references to the jackpot winner		
	Use of colloquialisms and slang		
	Use of Scots		
	Use of alliteration		

Now that you have analysed the differences, here are two important questions:

1 From your analysis, can you work out what differences there are in the readerships of the two types of newspaper?

2 What differences are there in the **purposes** of the two kinds of newspaper (i.e. what are they hoping to do for their readers)?

To simplify this task, if you want to use it, here is a list of possible purposes. Taking each one in turn, put a T (for Tabloid) if you think it is more likely to be a tabloid; or a B for Broadsheet.

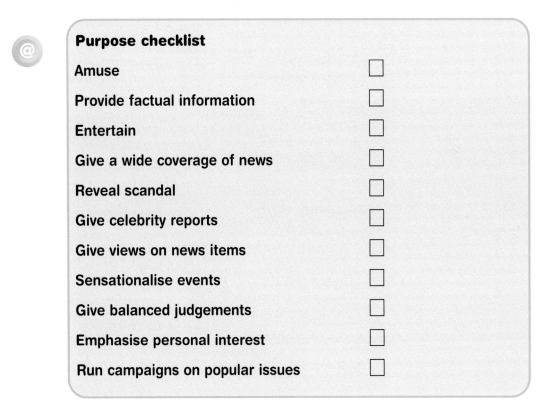

Purpose checklist

Amuse ☐

Provide factual information ☐

Entertain ☐

Give a wide coverage of news ☐

Reveal scandal ☐

Give celebrity reports ☐

Give views on news items ☐

Sensationalise events ☐

Give balanced judgements ☐

Emphasise personal interest ☐

Run campaigns on popular issues ☐

Finally, go back to the dictionary definitions of 'tabloid' and 'broadsheet' at the start of this section. Add two sentences to each definition from what you now know about them. You can also alter the original definitions if you don't think they are good enough.

You can practise writing in the style of a newspaper report by drawing on the stories you are reading. On the **Turnstones website** you will find a chapter of a book about which a pupil of your own age wrote the following broadsheet report.

Civil Unrest In Greenyards

The recent history of the clearances that have taken place in the Highlands to make way for sheep has been added to with the news that the residents of Greenyards are next in line for eviction.

The inhabitants of this close-knit farmland have dreaded this development for some period of time, but even so, it is still believed to be a severely distressing time for the majority of the Highlanders involved.

One young Greenyards resident, Connal Ross, stated: 'We first found out about our eviction when my dear friend, Rory Ruadh showed me an article that was featured in *The Berwickshire Gazette* claiming that our precious farms were to be let out. This upset everyone in Greenyards greatly, including myself. We have been aware for a long time that this development has been likely, but now that it has eventually happened we are extremely worried about what will happen next.

'I fear for some of the older residents of the village. They appear to be deeply aggrieved about the news and completely at a loss concerning their futures.'

The Highlanders claim that Mr. Alexander Munro, the holder of the main lease for Greenyards, swore that he would not sign any writs against them. This was said to have taken place on the 21st of March. What the Highlanders are apparently not aware of is that this information was misleading, for Alexander Munro did sign papers on the1st of March.

From that it could be concluded that in fact he did not break his promise as he resolved not to put his name to any writs that would be signed against them, suggesting an event to take place sometime in the future. This has outraged many of the Greenyards inhabitants because they feel as if they have been betrayed by Mr Munro.

After a failed attempt to serve writs, a second attempt was made by Sheriff-Officer Dugald McCaig. McCaig, allegedly under the influence of alcohol, was said to have been shouting insults at what seemed like everyone and anyone in Greenyards on his arrival at the village.

He is said to have threatened the elderly Mrs. Ross, Connal's mother, with a pistol. Local residents were said to have been utterly horrified at the Sheriff-Officer's conduct towards Mrs. Ross and other elderly residents.

It has been alleged that Connal Ross, in retaliation, drew a pistol and threatened McCaig. Witnesses stated that it was evident that the young man, desperate to protect his family, only did this in the defence of his mother who was paralysed with fear.

The residents of Greenyards have complained bitterly about the incident and have stated that they have the right to speak out in the proper defence of their right to remain on the land on which they were born and brought up. They believe that they speak for all the Highland farms attempting to resist eviction.

Extra challenge!

How do you know this is written for a broadsheet? What features does it have that tell you this?

Once you have worked out the challenge, the next task is to transform the article into a **tabloid version** of the same incidents.

In your groups, discuss how you might achieve this. Tabloids frequently dramatise stories, make up quotations and even tell lies about what has happened in order to catch the reader's interest. You can do the same!

Discuss what changes you will have to make, perhaps making a list of your thoughts. Now peel off to tackle the task on your own.

Afterwards, read each other's efforts and agree – if you can – on who is the best tabloid journalist. Maybe there's a career waiting! You might want to visit these websites to help you.

www.newspapers.com

www.newspapers.freeserve.co.uk

Why don't newspapers report in Scots?

Look back again at the two reports on the lottery winner. In pairs or groups discuss these questions:

1 Which report gives you the more vivid idea of the lottery winner's
   (a) actual expression of pleasure at winning the lottery?

(b) range of emotions?

(c) personality?

2 Does the reporting of his **speech in a Scots dialect** (instead of English) increase or decrease our understanding of these three things?

3 Why then do newspapers, especially local or Scottish national newspapers, not do full reports in Scots?

Our view is that our local and Scottish national newspapers should be much more **bilingual**, with reports and articles in Scots and English. We think that there is also a case for them being **trilingual**, reporting in Gaelic as well as Scots and English. And could they not also include news in Hindi-Urdu so that people originating from the Indian subcontinent would have access to information? It would certainly make both the broadsheets and the tabloids far more interesting. What do you think?

It wouldn't be a new thing! Less than 100 years ago Scots was used regularly in newspapers. Opposite is Jean Mcfarlane writing in the *Weekly News* on January 13 1906 about the scandal of women not being allowed to vote. The General Election was to be held the next day and she doesn't pull her punches! Yet it was to be another 22 years before women got the vote.

Here's the challenge. Turn this into a listening exercise. Shut your book and listen to your teacher read Jean Mcfarlane's article to you. With the help of others in your group, your job is to note down as many of the arguments as you can for women getting the vote. To give you a fair chance, your teacher will read the article twice.

Afterwards put your answers aside and read the article for yourself. Were your earlier answers right? Did you miss any of the arguments when you were listening that you can now see by reading?

'Jean M'Farlane on Voteless Weemen.'

Weekly News, January 13 1906

Oor mere men buddies in their wise stupidity hae declared that weemen shall hae nae vote, which, in my opeenion is aboot the biggest piece o' arrant nonsense an' rank injustice ever recordit in oor history.

Hoo should weemen no' hae a vote as weel as men? That is a puzzle whilk has bothered me for mony a day. What wad this boasted Empire o' oors, or the wide world aither, be withoot the guidin' wisdom o' weemen, eh? No' up tae verra muckle I'm dootin'.

Weemen even at praisent rule the warl', but, oh, at what a loss, for they hae tae dae sae in a seeckond-handit kind o' way. They hae first o' a' tae rule their men, an' then let the men try on their haun's at the rulin' o' the world, whilk unco affen, they mak' a gey puir job o...'

There's a wumman I am unco weel aquaint wi whase husband ackually drank himsel' intae his grave, leavin' his weedie wi' a helpless femmily o' seven, a rickety coal cairt, an' an auld horse the same as gin it had been made in a cooper's shop.

That puir wumman took up the management o' a business whilk wis scarcely worth a docken, but, bein' a contractor's dochter, she kent a' aboot horses an' cairts, an' to manage an' a' the rest o't.

Weel, settin' a stoot he'rt till a stey brae, she stairted wi' that auld coal cairt an' the dune auld horse, an' she stack in till she gat a new horse an' cairt. Syne she gat twa horses, an' syne she gat three. She gat employment an' guid wages tae men, keepin' their wives an' weans in comfort an' independence, an' at this present m'mment she has atween thretty and forty horses, an' abune a score o' men workin' till her, an' dependin' on her tae find wark for them tae gie them their weekly wages.

The mere men buddie governors o oor nation hae decreed that a' thae men are entitled tae hae a vote in the government (guid or bad) o' oor country, but they likewise hae declared that their employer – because she is a wumman – shall hae nae vote.

Oh, wives, did ye ever hear o' sich nonsensical tomfoolery, eh? I'm thinkin' no. That wumman gies over a hunner pounds a year tae the sae-ca'd Government o' this country in rates an' taxes, an' yet hasna a single say in whaur it is tae gang or hoo it is tae be spent or squandered.

From **The Language and the People – Scots prose from the Victorian revival**
by William Donaldson (Aberdeen University Press, 1989)

Here's an afterthought for your group to discuss: if newspapers today included articles written like that, would your mothers be keener to read them?

Some Scots words and phrases *do* get through into today's newspapers. Here are some examples:

1 'A bit less of the big gallus wummun persona would let Elaine C Smith's undoubted talent shine.' *(Scotsman* article.)

2 'This tastes boggin.' (HEBS anti-smoking advert.)

3 'It's a sair fecht when one has to watch one's Ps and Qs in one's own parliament, but it seems not only is one not allowed to raise one's own taxes, neither can one speak in oor ain mither tongue.' Well, only after it has been translated into the Queen's English or so it seems. *(Scotsman* reporting on a ruling that questions in the Scottish Parliament could be tabled in Scots only if accompanied by an English translation.)

4 'Jings man, dae ye no read yer Bible?' (from a *Scotsman* column, otherwise in English).

Can you think of a reason why the writers used Scots, or bits of Scots, in each of these texts? Here are some possible answers:

• simple accuracy (e.g. quoting a Scots speaker)

• to surprise the reader, as a contrasting change of register

• humour

• because it relates to a Scottish issue.

Finally, we invite you to express *your* conclusions about the whole issue of Scots in newspapers. You can do so in either Scots or English. Write your ideas in the form of a letter, either:

(a) to your local newspaper, demanding bilingual or multi-lingual reporting; or pouring scorn on that idea;

or:

(b) to the Executive of the Scottish Parliament, arguing for Scots to become one of its recognised languages (as Gaelic is).

Eftir aw that, ye kin haud yer wheesht.

13 Fun challenge: neologisms

Glossary

Neologisms
New words.

Onomatopoeia
The sound of the word suggests its meaning.

Derivation
The word in another language from which the English or Scottish word came.

Proper noun
A noun that is the name for a particular person, object or place, e.g. Harry, Shetland, McDonald's.

Common noun
A noun that is the name for an everyday object, person, idea or feeling, e.g. table, footballer, success, terror.

A language needs words for all the things that are important to the people that speak it. So new inventions, discoveries and ideas need new words. Where do these words come from?

Imagine you have invented something new and clever and useful. You will have to describe what it does, what's new about it and make up a name for it.

To make up a new word for your invention you could do one of the following:

- give your name to your invention
- use words from another language
- use old words in a new way
- use existing words to describe what your invention does
- use bits of existing words
- invent a new word, perhaps an **onomatopoeic** one.

These are all ways in which new words have come into languages in the past and continue to do so every day. We'll look at some of these ways in more detail. You'll need a good dictionary that gives **derivations** (where words come from). The derivation of a word usually appears in square brackets at the end of the entry.

Proper nouns that have become common nouns

When a person's name is used for the object or idea he or she has invented or discovered, a **proper noun** becomes a **common noun**. There are many famous examples. For instance, the word hoover is used for any vacuum cleaner and not just the ones invented by Mr Hoover. We write the word without a capital and we also use the word as a **verb** (to hoover).

Dyson may have overtaken Hoover as the most up-to-date vacuum cleaner, but note that you would still talk about 'hoovering with a Dyson' not 'dysoning'!

The sandwich is 'said to be named from the fourth Earl of *Sandwich* (1718–92) who ate a snack of this kind in order not to have to leave the gaming table'. Probably it should have been named after his servant instead! Again, this is a word which we now use as a **verb** as well as a **noun**.

Use the dictionary to find another five examples of individual people whose names have become words in the English language. Which words did these people coin?

- Captain Charles Boycott
- Sir Robert Peel
- James Watt
- Joszef Laszlo Biro
- Theodore Roosevelt
- Samuel Morse
- John Duns Scotus
- John Macadam
- Earl of Cardigan.

Words from another language

This is one of the most common ways for a language to find new words for new things. Think of food. When we try foreign food we are likely to use the foreign words for what we are eating, and for different methods of preparing and cooking food.

Which languages do you think the following words came from?

- cuisine
- puree
- casserole
- braise
- omelette
- baguette
- café
- restaurant
- chef
- champagne

- quiche
- spaghetti
- pasta
- pizza
- lasagne(a)
- macaroni
- cappuchino
- pakora
- samosa
- poppadom

- tikka
- tandoori
- kedgeree
- chop suey
- dim sum
- wok
- foo yung
- char siu
- tea

Scientists often use Latin and ancient Greek words to make up new words for new inventions and discoveries. Look up radio, thermostat, telephone and microbiology in a dictionary and find what languages give us these words. Latin and ancient Greek are languages, no longer in regular use. Why do you think we have used them to name so many modern inventions?

Old words with new usages

Many new ideas and inventions can be named by using old words in a new way. This is a bit like a writer using a metaphor. We might see a similarity between the new invention and an old familiar thing, and use the same word for both.

Why do you think a computer mouse is so-called?

Look up the following words to find their original, now mostly forgotten, meanings:

- benchmark
- watershed
- yardstick
- hallmark
- talisman
- horsepower.

Words made up from existing words

The users of some languages seem to prefer to make up new words by putting together existing words that describe the new invention or what it does. The German word for television is *fernseher* ('far-seer') and the word for the telephone is *fernsprecher*. Guess what that means.

In Norwegian the word for a vacuum cleaner is *stoorsuiker*. If you speak Scots, you'll know that *stoorsuiker* describes exactly what a vacuum cleaner does.

Some older British people still refer to the radio as the wireless. Can you find other words in English like these?

Words made out of bits of existing words

Acronyms seem to be very popular in English nowadays. You make up a new word by using the initial letters of other words. A famous example might be **posh**. The *Chambers 20th Century Dictionary* says: 'supposedly made from the first letters of the phrase

port   **o**ut   **s**tarboard   **h**ome

In the olden days people used to travel by sea rather than aeroplane. This phrase referred to the most desirable position of cabins when sailing to and from the East before the days of air-conditioning, but no evidence has been found to support this.

Find out what phrases give us these acronyms:

- laser

- radar

- AIDS.

Sometimes a **syllable** from each word is used to make up a new word. For example:

- Gestapo came from the German word **gesta**t **po**lizei, which means state police

- camcorder came from **cam**era re**corder**

- Nylon came from the names of two cities – **New Y**ork and **Lon**don.

Invented words

Brand names of products are frequently invented. Often these names become common nouns and we use them without thinking of them as names. Here are some examples; add some of your own.

- coke (from Coca Cola)

- iron brew (from Irnbru)

- cornflakes

- typex

- kleenex

- levis

- chinos

- sellotape.

Do any of your examples seem to have been created using **onomatopoeia**? Can you see why the companies that produced the following products thought these particular names would be good for sales?

- Fanta

- Snickers

- Crunchie

- Nike

- Bakelite

- Brillo

- Kitkat

Besides brand names, there are a few famous examples of words which were invented by an individual and that have come to be accepted and used like any other word. The word for inventing a new word is 'coining'. Can you explain why we use this expression?

Use the dictionary to find out who coined the word 'chortle'.

Neologisms in Scots

Minority languages are often accused of having no 'modern' words. It is pointed out that a great number of the words in the Scots dictionary are farming words belonging to a way of life which has mostly passed. Will there be new Scots words for our new lifestyle?

There is a famous story of a Gaelic speaker who was asked the Gaelic word for television. He replied by asking what the English word was. Which language gives us the word television?

Look at this list:

English	television
French	télévision
German	Fernseher
Spanish	televisión
Portuguese	televisão
Gaelic	telebhisean
Scots	television

What comments would you make?

Is television a Scots word? Look it up in a Scots dictionary. Why is it not there?

Some Scots language activists would like to see Scots following the lead of German and other Germanic languages in making up new words. We've already seen that the Norwegian word for a vacuum cleaner could easily become a Scots word, stoursooker. In his Scots language science fiction novel, Matthew Fitt uses many such coinages:

- Incendicowp
- taxlowpers
- cyberjouker
- cloodkittlers
- blooter resistant
- plastipoke
- surveillance puggie.

Can you invent any new Scots words for twenty-first century inventions?

To see how Scots can be adapted to the electronic age, click on The Scots Speikers Curn, Glesca, wab-steid backin:

http://www.mlove.free-online.co.uk/

The mouse is a moose, of course, but they also use established Scots words like wab, steid, stravaig and haundle to create the neologisms that new technology requires.

14 INFORMATION

UNLOCKING THE TREASURE CHEST

READING FOR INFORMATION

Being able to research a topic is a very useful and important skill. If you and your teacher decide to work on this challenge, you will be able to use the research skills you learn not just in English, but in other subjects too.

Researching is a skill that you will use long after you have left school. When might you need to do this? Is there a particular job where these skills are important?

Research can be quite a tricky task but we are going to try to help you to meet this challenge, showing you how to avoid some of the pitfalls and traps which can make it difficult. All 'seekers after truth' need a map to give them an idea of where they are going. Your quest is just like searching for treasure in the jungle. Indiana Jones would not wander aimlessly around, hoping that he will find treasure in the depths of the next temple. He would have a very clear idea of what he was looking for and a rough idea of where he was going, even if he was not very certain about what he might find along the way. Some planning is required and strategies have to be worked out first.

We think you need a map and a little help.

We think that the best way to introduce you to research is to take you on a **guided search** first, before letting you loose on your own.

The research task is to find out more about a person who has influenced us. We think that his life has been unusual and that it would be interesting to people of your age. You already met him in ***Turnstones 1***. His name is **Benjamin Zephaniah**.

Here is another short poem written by Zephaniah.

> **W** I used to think nurses
> **h** Were women.
> **o** I used to think police
> **,**
> **s** Were men.
> I used to think poets
> **W** Were boring,
> **h**
> **o** Until I became one of them.
>
> From **Talking Turkeys** by Benjamin Zephaniah (Puffin, 1995)

We already knew a little about him, but we wanted to find out more so that we could write his **biography**.

What do you think a biography is?

Discuss this in class before going on with this chapter.

For a biography we must avoid a boring list of facts that interests nobody. A good biography brings the person to life and makes us care about what she or he has done. To start you off, we have tried to write a biography to give you an example of this kind of writing.

The main **purpose** of our biography is to **inform** and **entertain** the reader by describing a character whom we think is interesting and exciting. In other words, we like him and we want to put that over to our readers. We also want to **persuade** the readers that they might want to find out more about Zephaniah and read some of his work.

We had a very clear idea of our **audience**: **people of your age** and *not* adults. How well do you think we did? Once you have read our biography and talked about it, say how we could have made it better.

READING CHALLENGE

1 Read the biography below.

2 Tell your partner three interesting things which you found out from the biography.

3 Cluster into fours and take 3 minutes to decide what the *group* feels are the three most interesting ideas in the passage.

4 Compare your ideas with others in the class.

You might not have found the biography interesting. If this is the case, pick out the three most *boring* things in the biography. Remember, it isn't enough to simply say that you didn't like it. You must be prepared to give evidence for your views and say *why* you thought it was boring.

Our biography of Benjamin Zephaniah

Dr Benjamin Obadiah Iqbal Zephaniah, 1958–

Benjamin Zephaniah left school at 12 years old, hardly able to read and write. He is dyslexic. Even now he is a famous author, he is unable to write in a way which we would understand. His secretary is the only one who is able to make any sense of the way in which he spells words. And yet in 1988 he was shortlisted for a fellowship at Cambridge University and later for Oxford Professor of Poetry. How did this come about?

Benjamin was born in 1958 in England. He grew up in Handsworth, Birmingham with the nine other children in his family. It was at this time that his love of poetry began. He grew up listening to the oral Jamaican poetry that his parents told him. To this day he recites all of his performance poetry from memory.

He did not have a successful time at school. He found it very difficult to read and write and he was finally expelled – for 'redecorating' the toilets. He frequently got into trouble with the police. By the age of 14,

Glossary

Reggae
A style of Jamaican popular music that has a strong beat.

he was in borstal and then he was sent to prison for 2 years for a crime he did not commit. It was in prison that he nearly died of a lung infection. He was released from prison in 1979 and moved to London. He became a Rastafarian, a musician and a poet. He claims he was composing and performing poetry before he could really read or write.

He opened a bookshop and became a reggae DJ. He has appeared on television documentaries; has acted in BBC TV and radio plays and still performs his own work at gigs, festivals and charity events.

His style is a mixture of Black English and Jamaican. Here are a few lines from 'Dis Poetry' from the collection **City Psalms** (Bloodaxe Books, 1992).

'Dis poetry is like riddim dat drops
de tongue fires a riddim dat shoots like shots
Dis poetry is designed fe rantin
Dance Hall style, big mouth chanting.'

Benjamin is a vegetarian. His favourite foods are butter beans, chick peas, sweet potatoes and soya ice cream. He also loves his dreadlocks and calls his hair his own personal garden. He has been growing his hair since he was 11 years old. He keeps it very clean and is proud that it now reaches his bum. His favourite time of day is the evening, when he has the time to relax and think about his writing. Although he did not learn to read or write at school, he now regrets this and claims that reading is fundamental because it increases knowledge and when you have knowledge 'no sucker can pull the wool over your eyes'.

He claims to read on planes, trains and in the little boys' room. The most unusual place was up a ladder! To relax he likes to collect money and restore classic sports cars. The people he admires are Spike Milligan and Percy B Shelley. But mostly he loves his mum.

Although Benjamin dislikes what he calls 'career politicians' he feels very strongly about many social issues. Much of his writing is about inequality and injustice, wherever it occurs in society. The headline he would most like to read is that politics have been banned and music has taken over. He is a patron of – which means he gives his support to – many different causes, including:

- a Chinese women's refuge group
- Lifelines (Prisoners on Death Row); he helped some inmates write a book
- Blackliners (Black HIV and AIDS)
- VIVA! (Vegetarian International Voice for Animals).

He is even vice-president of Ponthir Cricket Club and sponsor of Central Park Girls Football Team.

He has published many books of poems, pamphlets, novels and even several plays. Books of most interest to teenagers would be:

Face (Bloomsbury, 1999). This is his first novel and tells the story of a young man whose life is completely changed when his face is badly scarred in a joyriding accident.

Refugee Boy (Bloomsbury, 2001). A sensitive and intelligent boy from Eritrea seeks asylum in Britain to avoid the civil war raging in his own land. But he does not always receive the welcome he thought he would, as he battles to survive a different kind of hostility.

Talking Turkeys (Puffin, 1994). A collection of poems which encourages readers to be kind to their turkey at Christmas.

Funky Chickens (Puffin, 1996). More poems on all sorts of issues close to young people: equality; racism; green issues and many others.

Here are some reading challenges which will help you to understand the **genre** of biography and the way it is put together.

Work in pairs with a photocopy of the passage and use your highlighting pens to do the following tasks:

1 Find three facts about Zephaniah that were put in because the writer thought they would interest a *young* audience.

2 If you had to give each paragraph a title, what would you choose? Once you have had a chance to compare your headings with the rest of the class, write your title above each paragraph. Would it be easier to understand the biography if the writer had put in headings like these in the first place?

3 Use these paragraph headings to make a **mindmap** of Benjamin Zephaniah's life.

4 Why do you think we put the paragraphs into this order?

Zephaniah's biography is the kind of end product that you are aiming for. Our biography could be better. How would you improve it? Remember that we were trying to:

- inform

- entertain

- persuade you that he is an interesting man.

Did we succeed?

15 INFORMATION

UNLOCKING THE TREASURE CHEST

Now we are going to go back to the beginning of the research journey to let you see how we ended up with the finished Zephaniah biography. We had to work hard at it, just as if we were going on a hunt for treasure. There were **four stages** in our quest. We will look at each of the four stages in the next four chapters.

Stage 1 – Preparing for the trip.
Stage 2 – Deciding where to find interesting information.
Stage 3 – Deciding what treasure to bring home.
Stage 4 – Presenting what we have found to our audience.

STAGE 1 – PREPARING FOR THE TRIP

Anyone who *really* wants to succeed needs to do a bit of planning first. Planning takes time and lots of people try to skip it. But if you don't know where you are going, you're liable to end up somewhere else!

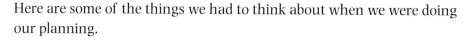

Here are some of the things we had to think about when we were doing our planning.

1 Who is our audience?

- people our own age?

- older people?

- younger people?

- people who are interested in our project?

- people who are not at all interested in our project and might need some convincing that it is important?

2 What is the purpose of our writing?

- to give information?

- to entertain?

- to persuade someone to continue our search?

- a mixture of all of these?

Once we had decided the answers to the first two questions, we then asked ourselves a third.

3 What is the *topic* of our search going to be?

Answering these questions means a lot of thinking, but it could save you extra work later. As with every quest, we knew that there would be difficulty, danger, exhaustion and a few pitfalls along the way.

PITFALL: A TRAP IN THE GROUND.

Glossary

Audience
The person or persons reading, watching or listening to the text.

Glossary

Purpose
The main intention or reason for doing something.

Once you have made up your mind about the three big questions we posed earlier, you *will* know what to do and you *won't* get lost. If you come up with some interesting ideas, people *will* care and they *will* enjoy what you have written.

Here are the answers to our three big questions.

Question	Answer
Audience	Young adults
Purpose	<ul><li>To give information</li><li>To entertain</li><li>To persuade young adults that Benjamin Zephaniah is interesting and worth reading about</li></ul>
Topic	A biography of someone interesting Benjamin Zephaniah

Do you think we need to add anything else to our planning at this stage?

Why do you think it was important for us to think about things like this first? After all, we were nowhere near ready to do any writing.

After our planning, we still had to start looking for information somewhere. But where?

16 INFORMATION:

UNLOCKING THE TREASURE CHEST

Glossary

Information
Knowledge transmitted and/or received, usually about a particular matter.

STAGE 2 – DECIDING WHERE TO FIND INTERESTING INFORMATION

So, we had done a lot of planning. We knew that we were looking for really interesting information on Benjamin Zephaniah, but where would we find it?

1 With a partner make a list of all the different places you could look.

2 After 3 minutes, group together into fours and see which group in the class can come up with the best ideas. There is no time to waste.

3 Here are one or two ideas to start you off. Copy the mindmap into your jotter and add as many good ideas as you can.

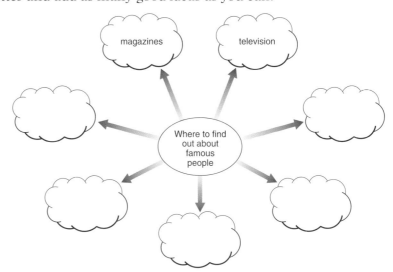

Once you have done this, turn over the page to see if you have a better list than we have.

Glossary

Abbreviations
A shortened form of a longer word, sometimes reduced to initials, e.g. DJ for disc jockey.

The Web
The World Wide Web (WWW) consists of interlinked sites on the Internet. Their texts are read by means of a browser and identified by an address called a URL.

Search engine
A program on the Internet that enables users to search for information.

 pages 81-83

WHERE CAN I FIND INFORMATION ON MY TOPIC?

- **Non-fiction texts** found in libraries. Each text tends to be about one particular subject or person and should contain true or factual information.

- **Reference texts** such as dictionaries and encyclopaedias. Great for shorter definitions and pieces of information.

- **CD-Roms** such as Microsoft Encarta. Similar to the paper version but much more fun to use, with lots of graphics and interactive activities.

- **The World Wide Web (WWW)**. What can we say? The world is at your fingertips! Beware though. There is a lot of useless information out there and it can be very time consuming sorting through it all.

- **Audio and visual media** such as the television and video. (Yes, now you can say you really are working whilst watching TV!) The news and documentaries are great for up-to-date information.

- **Newspapers, magazines and periodicals** are also good for current affairs, as well as interviews and opinions.

- **Other people** are the most invaluable resource we have. Don't forget to speak to people, such as your teachers, parents, school librarians, etc. Interviews and questionnaires can have very interesting results – **but only if you ask interesting questions**.

FINDING OUT ABOUT BENJAMIN ZEPHANIAH

Which questions do you think we should focus on when we are looking for information about BZ? (We will use this **abbreviation** as it takes a lot of time to keep writing Benjamin Zephaniah. It is often easier to use abbreviations when you are writing notes.)

Look back at our biography. Remember the paragraph headings you added? These might help you to think about the kind of questions we set out to answer. Would *you* want to find out anything else? Discuss this in pairs and then compare answers with the rest of the class.

We decided to go into the **Web** first and typed the words '*Benjamin Zephaniah*' into a search engine. A **search engine** is a magic program which will find information from all over the world on your topic.

Here are some **search engines** which were useful around the time when this book was printed. There may be some newer ones by now for you to try:

- www.google.com

- www.yahoo.com

- www.yahoo.co.uk

- www.excite.co.uk

- www.infoseek.com

- www.askjeeves.co.uk

WARNING! SPIDERS IN THE WEB!

Remember that you are being trusted to behave responsibly when you go onto the Web. There is some nasty stuff out there. Anyone can write anything on the Web and they frequently do! Most of the unsuitable sites will be filtered out by your school computer system. If you are irresponsible and try to go to these sites, you may lose the privilege of using the computers altogether. But also you are wasting time and you still have your challenge to complete. Stay focused on your task. You will find much more information than you can ever use.

We found the problem with the Web was:

To tackle information overload, we tried to stay focused on:

- our **audience** – young adults like yourself. One or two of the articles we found had things about the plays BZ had written for adults. We didn't think that our audience would be very interested in that. So we left them out.

- our **purpose** –
  to inform
  to entertain
  to persuade.

- our **topic** – we could get rid of lots of information at a glance because it was about BZ's music. Not what we were looking for. Lots of the information we turned up was on a prophet in the Bible called Zephaniah. This was not what we were looking for. We were also looking for information which was *reliable*. We looked for sites that we thought we could trust, like BZ's official website: (http://www.benjamin.zephaniah. com) We discarded information from less well known sites.

Remember, the Web isn't the only place to look! It's just that the Web has such masses of information and searching for something is fun! Whatever **sources** you are using, you need to keep the same things in mind.

We already mentioned that people are an invaluable resource. We got a really good piece of information from a friend who had listened to BZ talk at the **Edinburgh Book Festival**. She was the one who told us that BZ is dyslexic, which made us think again about the subjects of his stories and poems. We did check with BZ's agent to make sure this was true and to ask if we could use this information in our book. We were told that it was true, and that we could use it. Remember to try to check out your sources. If you can't check out to make sure they are true, then it might be best *not* to use what might only be gossip.

17 INFORMATION:

UNLOCKING THE TREASURE CHEST

STAGE 3 – DECIDING WHAT TREASURE TO BRING HOME

Now we get down to one of the hardest parts of this challenge. What do you do with all this information once you have found it?

You need to decide what to **select** and what to leave **behind**.

You need to learn and practise three strategies:

1 skimming

2 scanning

3 notetaking.

SKIMMING

When you read a text you should read through it first quite quickly. Don't worry too much about specific details or hard bits that you don't really understand. You are really just trying to get the gist or general idea of the passage. This is known as **skim reading**.

We are going to give you one of the Web pages that we found on BZ. Skim read over what it says. Now work with a partner and decide if it would be useful to you if you were writing the biography. Compare your ideas with the rest of the class.

Back to Index / Reader's Notes / Glossary

Benjamin Zephaniah
1958–

British / West-Indian performance poet and musician

Born in Birmingham and brought up in Jamaica, Benjamin Zephaniah spent time as a teenager in reform school and prison. It was largely due to these experiences that he embraced Rastafarianism, whose values inform his poetry. A musician and poet, Zephaniah has performed as a reggae DJ and worked in film, television and radio. He performs all his poetry from memory and maintains that he was composing and performing poetry before he could read or write effectively.

SCANNING

This is similar to skimming a text but you are reading it to locate a *particular piece* of information. To do this you skim over any irrelevant or unwanted parts of the text and look more closely at the part which contains the information that you want. You should **highlight** or <u>underline</u> important information so that you can find it easily when you start taking notes.

Work with a partner and look at the Web page again. Scan it for answers to these questions.

1 When was BZ born?

2 Where was he born?

3 What was interesting about his life as a teenager?

4 What does he do for a living now?

What bits did we think would interest you?

NOTETAKING

One of the difficult things once you have found your information is organising it so that you can use it easily later. We think mindmapping can help here. You might have worked out that the paragraph headings for our biography were:

- BZ's life story

- his interests

- his beliefs.

What do you think we were trying to do in the opening paragraph?

You might have decided on something different for your paragraph headings but you could still use these to help you draw a mindmap.

Put your topic in the centre. This is the focus of your map.

Group together other ideas and put them round the outside. It's easier to show you how to do it than to tell you.

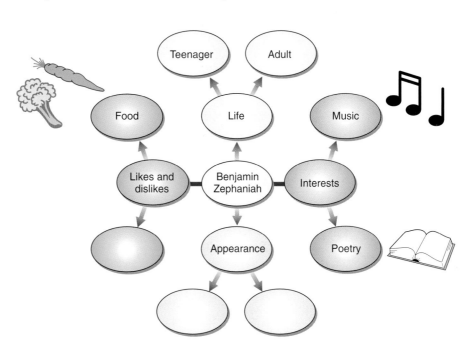

Look carefully at the map. Why do you think we have used different colours?

Why have we used symbols?

Did you work out that we used these symbols because BZ is a vegetarian who likes reading books and listening to music? Symbols sometimes make things easier to remember and colours help us to see that ideas from the same topic go together.

Now we are going to give you two other articles about Zephaniah. Your teacher will give you a photocopy of the passages. Work in pairs and highlight any information which you think would be interesting to your audience. We found it easier to look through both articles for information on the *same* topic, e.g. facts about his life. We used one colour of highlighter for this. Then we scanned for another topic and used a different colour for that. When you draw up your mindmap you can use the same colour coding for your bubbles.

Extract 1

Benjamin Zephaniah

I was not a great reader as a child. Most of the poems and stories I knew I heard from my parents. I grew up listening to a lot of oral poetry from Jamaica.

Reading is fundamental because it increases knowledge. When you have knowledge, no sucker can pull the wool over your eyes.

If you want to be a poet, read a lot, listen to poetry, be honest and true. Start writing from your own experiences.

I sometimes read on planes, on trains and in the little boys' room. The strangest place I ever read was up a ladder! At the moment my favourite of all my books is *Face* as it's my first novel.

To relax, I collect money and restore classic sports cars.

I admire Spike Milligan and Percy B. Shelley. But most of all I love my mum!

If you don't read, you are missing out on fun and ideas, many of which have changed the world.

From **http://www.rif.org.uk/word_fun/benzephaniah.htm**

The next extract is a bit harder, but we are sure you will be able to get something from it.

Extract 2

Benjamin Zephaniah

Benjamin was born in 1958 in Birmingham. He spent much of his early childhood on Fentham Road, Handsworth. He grew up in Handsworth with the other nine children in his family.

He was expelled from Broadway School for redecorating the school toilets, and got into frequent trouble with police. At the age of fourteen he was sent to borstal (reform school). Shortly after leaving he was fitted up and served a two year prison sentence for a crime he never committed.

Released after nearly dying in prison of a lung infection, in 1979 he moved to London, where he became active with the thriving late 70's workers co-operative scene. He set up a housing co-op and a bookshop. His first published pamphlet of poems, called 'Pen Rhythm', was published by Page One Books.

Through the dancehall and sound system scene he became involved in performance poetry. Articles then began to appear about him in the New Musical Express and Black Beat International, and a TV programme followed. In 1982, after extensive gigging in the UK and on the continent, he released the album RASTA.

In 1983 and 1985 favourite alternative London magazine 'City Limits' declared him 'Poet of the Year'.

In 1988 he was shortlisted for Oxford Professor of Poetry, losing to the future Nobel prize-winner Seamus Heaney.

Several TV documentaries followed.

In the last few years he has acted in BBC TV and radio plays, performed much poetry at gigs and festivals and charity events. BZ appears increasingly on radio and television as performer and cultural commentator. He still performs all his work from memory.

Among a variety of worthy causes, BZ is chairman of the Hackney Empire Theatre, and a patron of the Andrew Lee Jones Fund, which raises money to train new lawyers in capital defence work, and to provide scholarships for law students who want to work in the USA on behalf of those facing the death penalty.

From http://www.dabra.demon.co.uk/ben/benlife.html

Lastly, some pupils were lucky enough to have an interview with BZ. Here are the questions they asked and the answers he gave them.

Writer's block

What would make your perfect day?
Waking up surrounded by animals and jogging over the Welsh mountains, writing a great poem and a kiss before bedtime.

What would spoil your perfect day?
Seeing only humans and no other animal or nature. Being forced to spend most of my time in London.

What is your favourite food?
Butter beans, channa (chick peas), sweet potatoes, soya ice cream.

What food do you most dislike?
Any meat, I just don't like eating dead bodies.

Who or what do you most dislike and why?
I really dislike people who insist that their way is right and everyone else is wrong. I hate most career politicians.

Are there any missed opportunities that you wish you had taken?
I left school around the age of 12, I wish I hadn't.

What is your least favourite place to visit?
I like going to most places because it opens up the min going anywhere that is very cold.

What do you fear most?
Dis-United Nations.

If you had an epitaph written about you what would you like it to say?
He tried to luv everybody.

What is the worst job you've ever had?
Testing police whistles.

What age would you most liked to have lived in?
The beginning. In planning the future I would have left out war.

What time of day are you at your best?
Late night/early morning; there is peace and time for reflection and writing.

What's your cure for hiccups?
Kissing.

What's the worst thing about being male?
Not fully overstanding women.

The headline I would most like to read is ...
Politics is Abolished And Music Takes Over.

If grass wasn't green, what colour would you like it?
Red

From http://www.oneworld.org/zephaniah/block.html originally printed in **X5 Magazine Wales** and **World Beat** magazine.

DANGER ZONE

REMEMBER IT IS NEVER ENOUGH SIMPLY TO COPY AND PASTE INFORMATION INTO YOUR OWN DOCUMENT.

WHY? IT'S THE EASIEST THING TO DO AFTER ALL!

If you do this, the information will simply be going from the book or the computer onto your paper and into the teacher's hands without it ever having passed through your brain. The only way to learn from carrying out a project like this is to:

- try to make notes *only* on the information which you think will be interesting to *your* audience.

page 81

page 151

- do this in your own words. Don't just copy exactly what someone else has said. If you think their own words really are best, then you have to put inverted commas round the *exact* words they used. Look back at our biography for an example of how we did this. You might like to look at punctuation later in this book.

18 INFORMATION:

UNLOCKING THE TREASURE CHEST

STAGE 4 – PRESENTING WHAT YOU HAVE FOUND TO YOUR AUDIENCE

Just when you thought you were nearly there, we have another challenge for you. We have been taking you through the stages that we went through to write our biography of BZ. Now you are at the final stage.

Gather up your notes and decide:

- Which information is of most interest *to your audience?*

- Which information has potential but will need to be 'jazzed up' to make it more interesting to other young adults?

- Which information will be thrown away?

Pulling all the information together is like moving puzzle pieces about until a picture emerges. But instead of pieces, you are moving ideas and facts. It's a bit like finding your way through the jungle. Sometimes you get lost and disheartened, but you keep going.

BUILDING UP THE LIFE STORY

Some biographies present a long list of details and facts, strung out in a boring way like washing on a line. Your challenge is now to take the information which you organised on your mindmap and to blend the different items together into a series of well thought-out paragraphs which tell the really interesting stories.

So, get off the Web or close the book you are reading. Use your notes to create your own piece of writing. What do you think we focused on when we were doing this part of the challenge?

Try to remember what you thought we did well and the bits you thought could be improved in our biography.

Work with a partner and try to make a list of the things you should keep in mind when you are **drafting** a piece of writing and, in particular, a biography.

We tried to focus on the three big questions that we tackled at the outset of the challenge.

1 Who is our *audience*?
- people our own age?
- older people?
- younger people?
- people who are interested in our project?
- people who are not at all interested in our project and might need some convincing that it is important?

2 What is the *purpose* of our writing?
- to give information?
- to entertain?
- to persuade someone to continue our search?
- a mixture of all of these?

3 What is the *topic* of our search going to be?

CRITERIA FOR SUCCESS

In order to interest, inform and persuade young people about BZ, we felt we had to be careful how we organised the biography.

We felt that we had to:

- put our ideas in the best order (they could not be all over the place).

- make sure each topic had its own paragraph

page 138

page 151

page 156

- make the introduction grab the reader's attention
- have a conclusion that pulled the whole piece together and made the reader want to find out more
- use the best words we could think of and not just the first words which came into our heads
- think about how to use graphics, fonts and layout to make our biography look interesting
- use punctuation carefully and accurately to help our audience understand our biography
- check our spelling.

ARE YOU READY TO GO SOLO?

Now you are going to produce your own biography.

You could find out about someone from history, a hero or heroine, a famous person or someone close to you whom you admire.

Tom Cruise

Charles Darwin

Florence Nightingale

J K Rowling

You might want to find out about someone in your family and present them with a word processed and illustrated 'This is Your Life'. This could be a birthday or Christmas present that will save you a lot of money and is guaranteed to earn you lots of brownie points!

Think about what you have learned in your guided research. Can you remember the four stages? If you remember them, you will be able to do research and report writing in other subjects at school.

If you can't remember the stages, turn over the page now. 'Photograph' them in your mind's eye so that you have them ready whenever you need them.

STAGE 1

Preparing for the trip

- audience
- purpose
- topic

STAGE 2

Deciding where to go to find interesting information

- sources

STAGE 3

Deciding what treasure to bring home

- skimming
- scanning
- selecting
- notemaking

STAGE 4

Presenting what you have found to your audience

- drafting
- proofreading for accuracy

And now have a well deserved rest!

19 Unlocking persuasion: sooking up and sounding off

The whole of this next section is going to be about persuasion. If you have used **Turnstones 1** you will already have looked at some of the techniques used to persuade people. Don't worry, we are not going to go over the same old ground. But we are going to ask you to look at some things in a bit more *detail*, and you are going to find this section more challenging. That's the nature of English. You keep practising the same skills but you go deeper and deeper. It's like peeling an onion. You take off one skin in early primary and another later on. Even when you are very old, as old as your teacher, you still won't have reached the centre of your onion!

Persuasion is a very important skill to learn and to keep working at. As well as enabling *you* to persuade *others*, it helps you to recognise and to *resist* when other people are trying to persuade you to think or act in a certain way.

Why is resisting persuasion important?

We think it is important that you are able to decide for yourself. You shouldn't be led into doing something you don't really want to do or to be made to think in a certain way simply because someone else tells you to. What do you think?

Task

You are going to listen to or read two very different texts which are each trying to persuade the reader about something different. Your challenge is to think *how* they do this. You will be given a copy of the page to work on.

On page 109 you will find a table which you should copy and fill in with your notes. This will help you to see what techniques both writers use and which techniques are used only by one writer. Your teacher will tell you whether you should use the table at the start of the task or *after* you have looked at each text.

Your completed table will give you an at-a-glance summary of all of the strategies that you can use when you are trying to persuade. Keep it safe! It might help you also in modern studies or in history.

Text 1: sooking up

Your teacher will read this first text to you, pretending to be the speaker.

Listen carefully and ask yourself **how exactly does the girl persuade her Mum to buy her the new shoes?**

Work with a partner and write down your answers.

Now read the text by yourself and see if you can add to your answers.

With a partner highlight or underline all of the ways in which the girl tries to persuade her Mum to buy her the new shoes. You should be good at this as we are sure you have used the same techniques many times!

Mum can Ah get?

Mum, can Ah get that? Oh Mum, can Ah, please? Ah promise Ah'll be good. Ah'll no ask for anythin again. Oh please Mum, can Ah just have it?

It's no fair. Ah never get anythin. Dee-Anne gits whatever she wants. Ah never got anythin when she got her new shoes last week. Ah want a new paira shoes.

Oh look, Mum, those shoes are dead nice, in't they? Oh so ur they wans oer there. No they wans o'er there are nicer. Can ah get them Mum? They'd go nice wae ma wee black skirt. Oh Mum, Ah've got tae have them. Please. Ah'll be able tae wear them tae Nicole's birthday party the morra. Aw ma pals are getting somethin new tae wear. Oh please Mum, can ah get them?

Ah can! Oh great Mum! Ah'll no ask for anythin else. Ah promise! Ah'll still need to find a top tae wear. Ah'll probably have tae wear that auld cream top. Ah wish Ah had a new top tae wear ...

Text 2: sounding off

Read Mr Nairn's letter below. First skim read it to find out roughly what he is saying – to get the gist of the text.

page 93

What is he saying about teenagers in general?

Teenage hooligans

Nairn's Newsagent
Main Street
Hightown
PA6 7QT

12th July 2000

The Editor
The Sunday Record
Glasgow
G95 4PQ

Dear Sir,

I was delighted to read your article about young hooligans in last week's Sunday Record. I couldn't agree more. Young people of today are all layabouts, what with their mobile phones and Walkmans. It wasn't like that in my young day. We all had to work hard **and** for very little reward! We would never have given cheek back to our elders and betters. They are all lazy timewasters and what's more the only reason they come into my shop is to shop lift. I own a newsagents so I should know!! They would stick a knife into you as soon as look at you.

Keep up the good work. It is only by exposing their selfishness that they will learn to give people like me a bit of respect.

Yours sincerely,

John Nairn

- Now read Mr Nairn's letter more **closely** to pick out *exactly* what points he is making about teenagers. Do you agree with his points? Have a discussion in pairs or groups of four about this. Report back to the whole class not only on what you think about his points, but on how they make you feel.

● Read the letter *again*. This time you are going to be scanning for particular information. In the table below we list the various techniques Mr Nairn uses to persuade you. Your challenge is to find examples of each technique from his letter.

Technique used to persuade	Example
He uses insulting words.	'hooligans'
He makes sweeping generalisations which are not true in all cases.	
He is biased in favour of young people of his day.	
He states his opinion as if it were fact.	
He exaggerates.	
He flatters his audience.	
Any others?	

Passage	Techniques and strategies used	Example (You might not need to fill in this column if you think you can remember the techniques. Ask your teacher what to do.)
Mum can Ah get		
Teenage hooligans		

Which of the two texts did you think was most effective at persuading the target audience to agree with the views given? You might have a group or paired discussion about this but remember to give reasons for your views.

Writing and talking challenges

Here are some individual or partner challenges for you. Your teacher will help you to decide which ones to do. We don't think you will want or need to do all of them!

1 Improvise a dialogue, i.e. a conversation, between an adult and a child. The child is trying to persuade the adult to buy him or her something. What might that something be? Look back at your techniques grid and use some of the strategies that you noted there.

2 'Mum can Ah get' is a monologue. That means it is a text, in this case written down, where only one person's thoughts are made known to the reader. It is like listening to one side of a telephone conversation. The reader has to guess what the other person is saying. Write down one part of the dialogue that you improvised above to make a monologue. How can you make it sound realistic? Look again at 'Mum can Ah get' for some ideas on how to do this.

page 31

3 What school issue do you feel strongly about? Whom do you want to persuade? How will you make your views known? Will you give a talk at a school assembly; write a letter to the head teacher; produce a pamphlet or flyer to be given out to pupils; record a broadcast for the school radio; or set up a Web page inviting others to write in? What is the best **form** for your persuasion to take for it to have most chance of succeeding?

However you do it, remember:
- your challenge is to persuade
- you need to think who you are trying to persuade *and* how best you can persuade them.

4 Think about Mr Nairn's letter. How would you like to reply to him? What form would be most effective? A letter to the same newspaper; a videoed reply to watch on his TV; a multi-media presentation to look at on his computer; a poster to be stuck on the window of his shop? Use similar techniques to those employed by Mr Nairn. Look back at what you noted on your grid. Your challenge – and it is quite a challenge – is to persuade him that teenagers are not a waste of space.

5 You are going to be like Mr Nairn; totally over the top and outrageous in your views on a topic of your choice. You are going to practise being prejudiced and giving views which you cannot possibly support with evidence! By doing this you will learn that it is not a very effective way of persuading your audience because you upset more people than you persuade. Also, if you give them inaccurate or wrong information, they will not trust your viewpoint in the future. They might even think that you are not quite right in the mind.

What is your topic going to be?

- Perhaps that much needed savings could be made in the National Health Service if all people over the age of 40 were simply done away with. This would also lead to far more opportunities for bright young things like you.
- Perhaps that girls should never, under any circumstances, be allowed to wear trousers to school.
- Perhaps something equally or more outrageous.

Remember, you can be as over the top as you like. However, bear in mind that swearing is *not* an effective way of communicating. It simply shows that you have a very limited vocabulary and alienates the people you want to persuade. You are trying to *impress* people with your persuasive powers.

You might decide to deliver a very persuasive **talk** rather than a piece of writing. If so, you will have to decide what kind of body language you are going to use.

- Are you just going to stand there looking down at your paper, with your hands in your pockets? How persuasive is that?
- Watch some presenters on television. Note what they **do**, as well as what they **say**, to try to persuade you.
- Which programmes might be good to watch to learn how to do this? That's a bit of a novelty, telling your parents you have to watch television for homework!

20 Unlocking persuasion: hard facts and sound sources

You can be very persuasive without resorting to Mr Nairn's techniques. People can usually see through misinformed arguments like his and many would simply dismiss him as a nutter. You don't want people to do this to you, so you have to be clever about persuading. This section will show you how.

Choosing a cause

Sometimes we feel very strongly about an issue and we want others to know how we feel. So, what really interests you, angers you or makes you particularly sad?

> **A recent survey by the Department for International Development found 70 per cent of 11–16-year-olds were worried about world poverty. Amnesty International (http://www.amnesty.org) says 400 schools have signed up to its human rights programme and more are in the pipeline.**
>
> **(*Times Educational Supplement Scotland*, 02.06.2000).**

Some teenagers like you were asked what campaigns they felt most strongly about. Here are their top ten.

1 Direct action to stop genetically modified foods.

2 Mahogany is murder – campaign to protect UK's wildlife habitat and the world's forests.

3 Factory watch – expose your local polluters.

4 Disarming of child soldiers.

5 Children's rights in the UK – particularly thinking of asylum seekers.

6 Foxhunting and live animal transport bans.

7 End battery hen and fur farming.

8 Campaign against cosmetic testing.

9 Protect the Amazon.

10 End commercial whaling.

Are some of your favourite causes listed? If not, here are some other controversial topics (and I am sure you can add more):

- Why are boys not doing as well as girls at school?

- Should books or films be censored if they are unsuitable for certain age groups?

- Should the following be banned:
  - fireworks?
  - mobile phones at school?
  - collecting things, such as Pokémon, beanies?
  - playing with guns?
  - all 'sports' which exploit animals?

- Should all pupils be taught in the same schools, no matter how rich they are or what their colour, creed or religion is?

- Should children who have a physical or mental disability be taught in mainstream schools?

- Should Siamese twins be separated if it means that one will die in order to save the other?

- Should countries like Britain welcome refugees and asylum seekers?

- Should people be able to buy babies on the Internet?

- Should people who are terminally ill or severely handicapped be allowed or even helped to die?

- Do schools and society do enough to combat bullying?

- Should there be an early evening curfew on teenagers?

- Should people be allowed to keep dogs which are dangerous, e.g. pit bull terriers?

- Would you support campaigns on vandalism, litter, pollution or for building new schools?

Carry out a survey to find out which issues are the top ten concerns of your class. You could encourage other classes to do the same. Think how you could display your findings. You could record your results as a poster for the wall, as a pie chart or bar graph like those you use in maths or geography.

Your views on these issues are probably based on **beliefs** and **feelings**, not on **facts**. You might be able to persuade others just by expressing your beliefs and feelings with enough force – but they would be stupid to believe you. They should only be persuaded by hard facts, and you need reliable sources for these facts. This next section aims to help you to think about **fact** and **opinion**.

Glossary

Source
The person or organisation who originally supplied the information

Whose views can you rely on?

The task

Compare the following **editorial** and letter by highlighting the *facts* and, in a separate colour, the *sources* for the facts. However much you share the beliefs and feelings of the writers, which text is more convincing **according to the facts they present?**

Take one text at a time: first the **editorial**.

Editorial: Wish he wasn't there

Picture the scene. After months of hard slog and dismal weather, you've finally got away on holiday. The stress of exams, mates and boys seem a million miles away, as you lie back and enjoy the exciting experiences of an idyllic foreign land. But with different sights and sounds comes a different culture and, as you walk through the streets of your holiday destination, you're certain to stumble upon new experiences. A baby bear, muzzled and attached to its owner by a lead, may seem like a heartwarming sight as it dances for the crowd. You may even be tempted to give the owner a little of your holiday money – after all, a dancing bear is more entertaining than a busker singing some duff song you've never heard of. But are you sure it's really a good idea?

Dancing bears

Of course it's tempting to stop and watch. But not when you hear what many of the bears have been through to make them perform. With the holiday season upon us, it's worth thinking about what's going on away from the sandy beaches and hotel rooms of some of our favourite holiday destinations.

'Bear cubs are beaten with sticks to make them stand upright and appear to be dancing,' says Jonathan Owen, of the World Society for the Prevention of Cruelty to Animals (WSPA). 'Or they are placed on metal trays over burning embers while music is played – so the bear associates pain with music and picks up its feet whenever it hears it.'

In the big cities of Greece, Turkey and Bulgaria, dancing bears are common. Bear cubs are taken from their mothers, who are often shot dead. The cubs then have a hole drilled through their noses, so a chain can be inserted to pull them around. This treatment has outraged many locals, who grew up seeing bears on the street but had no idea of the cruelty involved. With the help of tip-offs and the co-operation of the Turkish Tourist Board, the WSPA has saved many bears.

'Knowledge is a powerful tool,' says Shelley Simmons, from campaign group the Animal Defenders.

'When people hear the facts, they're horrified.'

Isn't he cute

You might be outraged by fox hunting and badger baiting in Britain, but when you're in holiday mode it's easy to be blind to what's going on.

From Bliss (July 2000)

Thinking challenge

Work in pairs for this task. Take 3 minutes.

- Are there a sufficient number of facts in the editorial to convince you?

- Are the sources of these facts likely to be reliable?

- Does this article make you think about how animals are treated?

- Does it make you agree with the author that you should not encourage this kind of thing?

- How does it do this? Is it effective?

Now compare the **editorial** with the letter given below. The letter was sent to the magazine in response to the editorial.

- Is the letter equally convincing?

- Check out the facts and the sources for the facts.

- How could it be improved?

You will probably have been asked to do this kind of task in history or modern studies. Try to remember what you have been taught in those subjects about *fact*, *opinion* and *reliable sources*.

Work in pairs for this task for 4 minutes. Cluster together into fours for another 4 minutes to share your ideas. Finally, be prepared to present your views to the rest of the class.

Letter to the editor

The Editor
Bliss Magazine
London
WC2H 8JG

Dear Sir,

I read your article on dancing bears (Bliss, June 2000) with great interest. Another cruel spectator sport is bullfighting. I think this 'sport' is disgusting. It exploits animals for fun and this is totally unfair and unjustified.

The animal has to endure excruciating pain until it suffers a long drawn out death – and this is supposed to be in the name of entertainment!

In 1993, a French poll found 83% of people were against bullfighting. Now many towns have been forced to stop putting on fights because of widespread opposition.

I do appreciate that in some areas bullfighting has a long tradition and that it is part of Spanish culture. But, I feel that there should be no place for it in today's society.

Yours sincerely,

Sophie Hall

page 91

Glossary

Prejudice
Judgement or opinion which might not be based on the facts. This is usually written by someone who has a definite sympathy or dislike for a person or idea.

Bias
Not so strong as prejudice. Selection of information by someone who is inclined to favour one person or one side of an argument.

Writing or talking challenge

Choose a topic that you feel strongly about. How will you make your views known? Will you produce a video or audio tape, a letter or an article for a teenage magazine or the *Big Issue*, or a give-away pamphlet. Your **audience** is other young people, the same age as yourself.

Your challenge is to write or talk to persuade your audience to agree with your views. If you write a letter, you might want to send it to a magazine, or you could make up a class magazine of editorials, letters and articles on a variety of topics. Or you could give a starter talk for a class discussion or talk on one side of a formal debate.

Here are some useful websites. Remember to look for prejudice and bias.

- Amnesty International: http://www.amnesty.org.uk

- World Society for the Prevention of Cruelty to Animals: http://www.wspa.org.uk

Or you could type your topic into a search engine.

Remember

Television, radio, newspapers, magazines and websites are the kinds of places where you will find people expressing *their own* views. When you are listening or reading you need to be very careful to notice when people are giving *their opinion*. This may well be very biased. How can you tell when someone is giving a view which has been carefully thought out and has valid evidence to support it?

Planning your argument

Here is a writing frame to help you to get started. Although it is meant for writing, it could help you make notes for a talk. Just make sure you don't simply read your facts out.

State the problem and your point of view:

Points you want to make (assertions)	Evidence
1 Firstly I think that ...	
2 Secondly I feel that ...	
3 In addition it is obvious that ...	

Conclusion, summary or what you think should be done:
In conclusion I feel that ...

Fact and opinion: who says?

In the section on 'Sounding off' one of the writing challenges asked you to:

- present a **one-sided, biased viewpoint**

- give your opinion.

1 Can you think of a subject in school where it is important to be able to sort out *fact* from *opinion*, and to give an **unbiased viewpoint?**

2 Can you think of an occasion outside school when it is important for you to be able to do this?

page 107

One of the ways in which we try to persuade people is by **exaggerating** our opinion and by choosing *only* the evidence that *supports* our case. If you can't remember how this was done, look back at the **Teenage hooligans** passage to see how this works. It is important that you can spot when people are trying to persuade you in this way.

When we read and write about an issue, we need to be able to sort out what is fact and what is opinion. When is an author saying something that can be *proved* and that can be backed up by evidence; and when is he or she stating an opinion that is a private belief which cannot be proved or supported with evidence?

Here is another task to give you more practice in spotting the two approaches.

Some pupils were asked to write about a famous pop star or band. They had to say why they admired that star and they had to make their writing really interesting. Their challenge was to give information about their subject, but also to persuade their audience that their chosen singer or group was really interesting. You can see one result in Text 1.

Text 1: The FrontShop Boys

FrontShop Boys are the hunkiest group ever. Any other group is pants beside them. They sing good lyrics and are cool singers and dressers. They started as a boy band in Glasgow in 2001 and I think they are really ace! Charlie is my favourite. He went to school in Paisley and worked as a butcher for three years, singing part time before they made it big time. I have been to all of their gigs and any other group is just zero.

Another group of pupils was asked to write persuasively about a school issue about which they felt strongly. This is Text 2.

On your copy of Text 2 use different coloured highlighters to mark:

● what the writer feels strongly about

● each point she makes to try to persuade the reader

● the evidence she uses to support her argument.

Text 2: Trousers 4 girls

There are still many schools where girls are forbidden from wearing trousers as part of their uniform. I am sick of girls being discriminated against in this way. In school, teachers say that everyone is equal and that they should be treated the same. However, in this instance, girls are being discriminated against and the school uniform policy blatantly contradicts this statement.

Firstly, I feel that girls should be allowed to wear trousers because girls get cold too. The current fashion is that skirts should be worn really short. No-one would be seen dead in a long skirt. In winter, this means that we freeze to death or have to wear sticky, itchy tights, which are uncomfortable and expensive. And, if we don't wear tights, we have to shave our legs everyday or worse still, suffer the excruciating pain of having them waxed.

Secondly, trousers are much more practical. Have you tried running for a bus in a skirt? We are scared to bend down to tie our shoe laces in case perverts are trying to check us out. Furthermore, going up and down stairs and sitting down is a total nightmare. If we wear short skirts, parents and teachers are constantly on our backs saying that our skirts are too short and reveal far too much. This problem of indecency could be solved at a stroke if only we were allowed to wear trousers.

On the other hand, the main argument against girls wearing trousers is that they are not smart or ladylike. However, I would maintain that this is the 21st century and trousers are being worn by women in all walks of life, in hundreds of countries all over the world. It is time education caught up. Come on girls! You have nothing to lose but your skirts!

Adapted from http://www.welcome.to/trousers4girls

Thinking challenge

What is the author of each text trying to do in their writing? Which one do you think does the job better? Have a class discussion about this. Remember you need to back up what you think with evidence.

page 91

Hint

Look at the parts of the text which you have highlighted. Can you pick out the evidence which is based on fact from the evidence which is based on opinion. Use a different colour or different kind of line to highlight interesting information.

Look again at Text 2:

● Whom do you think this was written for?

● Where might you find a text like this?

● How can you check up whether Text 2 is telling the truth?

● Can you use any of the strategies in Text 2 to persuade *your* reader or listener?

You might want to visit the website where we found Text 2. Decide whether it is an effective Web page or not.

● Is it well laid out?

● Is it persuasive?

Hint

When this book went to print Text 2 was on http://www.welcome.to/ trousers4girls. However, it might not be there now as this is the way with the Internet. Pages come and go. Some of them sit there for years and nobody does anything with them. They can become hopelessly out of date. Always try to find somewhere on the page to say when it was last updated – check that you are looking at recent information. You should also look to see if a Web page is likely to be a reliable source of information, or simply someone's opinion. There is more on this in the chapters on 'Information: unlocking the treasure chest.'

If you cannot get access to the Internet your teacher may be able to arrange to have Text 2 downloaded and printed off for you. You could design a Web page on a large sheet of A3 paper and use coloured Post-Its as your links.

21 Fun challenge: unlocking signs

Glossary

Sign
A simple public notice, with or without words, carrying a message, e.g. a street name, a road sign.

Symbols
A sign or object which stands for something, e.g. the logo on your trainers representing the company which makes them.

Much of what we have been looking at in this book has been to do with 'unlocking' texts. As you have discovered, there are many different types of text, not just the written word on a page. In this section you will find lots of different **signs**, **symbols** and messages. As a group answer the following questions for each sign. If you cannot figure one of the signs out think of how you can find out and do it as homework.

1 What am I? (e.g. road sign, advertisement, etc.)

2 What am I saying?

3 What is my purpose? (e.g. to inform, to warn, to command etc.)

4 How do I communicate that purpose? (e.g. symbols, colours, words etc.)

Once you have answered the four questions for each picture, you should group the signs into categories. You can do this in any way you like, perhaps according to purpose, message or type of sign. See how fast you can complete the exercise or how many you can get. Can you beat the other groups in your class? Have fun!

Hopefully this has been an interesting and challenging task for you.
Perhaps it has made you more aware of the signs and symbols that we see
in our everyday lives, and what they are telling us and why they are there.

22 Unlocking talk: it's not what you say, it's the way that you say it

We already know that, by looking at the language which other people use, we can tell when they are trying to persuade us or influence us. If we know the tricks of their trade, we can, when we wish, resist their influence. If we don't know the tricks and take what people say at face value, we will be like the dodo in Chapter 1, with no control over our future.

Most of this book has been about helping you to *recognise* these tricks. This section, and the next, is designed to help you *use* the tricks, to express yourself well in speech and writing.

The magic of language

To remind you just how clever language is, think about how animals have to communicate.

> If the cats could talk like us, the home cat might say, 'I saw you on my bit yesterday and I warned you then not to come back. I told you what would happen if you came back today. But you didn't listen, did you? Here you are again today. You're a meengy looking beast and I'm disgusted just by the sight of you. This is your last chance. Go now and don't come back tomorrow. If you do, you will get what is coming to you. On your bike!'

However, cats can only puff up their fur and caterwaul.

What do *we* need to do with this magical language stuff to make the best possible use of it?

Have a clear purpose

Unlike cats, we can use language to serve many **purposes**. For example, can you pick out from the home cat's imagined speech opposite where it used language in order to:

- describe what happened in the past?

- describe what might happen in the future?

- say how it feels?

- hurt the other cat?

- threaten and warn?

- order the other cat off?

- describe appearances?

Which of these would you say was the main *purpose* of the cat's language on this occasion?

With speech, this is often how we use language: we have a *main* purpose and we use lots of different tricks to persuade others to do as we want.

With writing it is a bit different. Most often, we have to decide what our **purpose** is for *each* **paragraph** and then stick to it.

So we can get away with much more in speech than in writing. If you think someone is trying to pull the wool over your eyes, say, 'Put it in writing.' Then you'll be able to see what they are up to!

Be aware of your audience

We need to change our language to suit our purpose, but also to suit our **audience**. What has gone wrong with the following attempt to talk casually about the weather?

- What is strange about the girls' conversation in this context?

- What would you think of people who speak like these two all the time?

- When would we expect to hear language like that of the second girl?

- Who would be using it?

- What would be the purpose of using it?

- Who would the audience be?

Now write your own, more appropriate, reply to the first girl's statement about the weather.

Use the right genre

Changing your language to suit your audience and purpose will lead you to talk or write in a particular genre. You can see the difference in the genre between the two girls talking about the weather. Tease out what the differences are between the genre of casual conversation and that of the technical weather forecast. You should consider differences in:

- formal and informal ways of speaking
- dialect and non dialect
- technical and non-technical vocabulary
- simple, compound and complex sentences.

Genre differences are generally easy to see. Sometimes we call them **genre markers** because they are the features which mark one kind of text as being different from another. Every type of talk or writing has its own genre. Think how a recipe is different from a diary, and how a science report is different from a poem.

Here is a task to see if you can spot genre markers. On the next page there is a text with a picture of the Scottish runner Liz McColgan. The picture is taken from a newspaper account of her victory in a long-distance race. But you will very quickly realise that the page is not from a newspaper, but from a school textbook. Your task is to decide for which school subject it is written. Justify your answer by identifying as many **genre markers** as you can for books written for that subject.

How do cells use food?

Glucose is our body's main 'fuel'. We use it to release energy in a process called respiration.

Figure 1 Exercising muscles need more energy.

Figure 2 Glucose is our main source of energy.

On supermarket shelves you can see many high-energy foods and drinks. People like them if they are playing energetic sports or even if they are having a busy day and need a bit of extra get up and go. Energy is needed for all the reactions that are happening in your body. New cells need to be made for growth. Old cells need to be replaced. Chemicals have to be made and moved from one place to another. Your body temperature has to be kept normal. The more we exercise, the more energy our muscles need to be able to contract. If we are very ill and cannot eat, then we may need to be 'fed' by putting a solution of glucose straight into our bloodstream.

Glucose is a high-energy chemical and is our main fuel. The energy released from it is transferred and used in different ways in the body. But how does this happen? Glucose doesn't provide energy in a tube of tablets in your pocket. The energy is locked into the tablet and has to be released.

Small glucose molecules are produced when carbohydrate (see page 8) from foods like bread and cereal is **digested**, or broken up, by **enzymes** in the small intestine. Energy is released from glucose in the cells in our bodies in much the same way as energy is released from other fuels. Fortunately for us, however, glucose does not catch fire! If there is a plentiful supply of oxygen, energy is released from glucose and carbon dioxide is produced. This reaction is called **respiration**. A simple equation for the reaction is shown below. When it happens in our cells it is called **cellular respiration**.

Although respiration can be shown by one equation, the breakdown of glucose in cells really takes place in a series of small steps. Each step is made possible by the action of enzymes. In all tissues in the body the overall reaction uses the glucose produced by digestion of food molecules to release energy.

glucose + oxygen → carbon dioxide + water + ⟨ENERGY TRANSFER⟩

Dialect and Standard English

An awareness of audience is needed when we are deciding whether to speak in **dialect** or **Standard English**. Whether we like it or not, people make assumptions about us from the way we speak and write. Their attitudes can be unreasonable and inconsistent; an employer who speaks in dialect most of the time may, nevertheless, expect interviewees for a job to be able to speak Standard English. Sometimes we can see the sense in this – perhaps the employee has to speak to customers from all parts of the UK on the telephone; some customers might not be able to understand the local dialect.

But language choice is not just about getting a job when you are grown up. You will often meet and speak with people you don't already know. Sometimes they might come from another part of the UK or even from another part of the world. Speaking to them in your own dialect won't work – you will not be understood. And people will think you are stupid for not realising this. They expect you to adjust to Standard English which is the only dialect (yes, Standard English is a dialect too) which everybody can understand.

Even in your own family you may sometimes have to adjust. Here is a poem by Jackie Kay about such a situation. The girl in the poem thinks her English cousin is a snob. But is she really? Read the poem and have a class discussion about who is to blame for the disagreement.

English cousin comes to Scotland

See when my English cousin comes,
It's so embarrassing so it is, so it is.
I have to explain everything
I mean Every Thing, so I do, so I do.
I told her, 'know what happened to me?
I got skelped, because I screamed when a skelf
Went into my pinky finger: OUCH, loud.
And ma ma dropped her best bit of china. It wis sore, so it wis, so it wis.
I was scunnert being skelped
When I wis already sore.
So I ran and ran, holding
My pinky, through the park.
Over the burn, up the hill.
I was knackered and I fell
Into the mud and went home

Mocket and got skelped again.
So I locked myself in the cludgie
And cried, so I did, so I did,
Pulling the long roll of paper
Onto the floor. Like that dug Andrex.'
Whilst I'm saying this, my English cousin
Has her mouth open. Glaikit.
Stupit. So she is, so she is.
I says, 'I'm going to have to learn you
What's what.' And at that the wee git
Cheers up; the wee toffee nose says,
'not learn you, teach you,' like she's scored.

From **Two's Company** by Jackie Kay (Puffin, 1994)

You could work in twos this time and, taking parts, read this poem out loud.

- How will you divide it up?

- How will you read your part?

- Which pair can perform it best?

To do this well you need to think a bit about the following questions:

1 How does the girl feel about her English cousin? Why is this?

2 How do you think the English cousin feels about being in Scotland?

3 How does she feel about her Scottish cousin?

4 Would the English cousin understand what her Scottish cousin was saying? Which words might she find difficult? Do you understand what they all mean?

5 Do you think the English girl in the poem is a snob because of the way she talks?

At the end of the task, decide what advice you would give to each of the girls to help them first to understand each other and then to become friends. We think that the advice to the Scots girl should be in Scots. What do you think?

We think it is important that we are **bilingual**. By this we mean that it is important that we can move confidently from dialect to Standard English. We might choose to speak in dialect when we speak to our own friends. But, we also need to be able to speak in Standard English when we are in a formal situation.

Elvish dialect

Here is another example your teacher might want you to look at. In this book the author makes her characters use dialect to reveal something about their characters. Winky and Dobby are house elves at Hogwarts, the magic wizarding school attended by Harry Potter.

Your teacher will read the extract out loud to you. As you listen, think about the kind of people Winky and Dobby are and the relationships they have with the others in the extract – Harry and Hermione.

'You is ought to be ashamed of yourself, Dobby, talking that way about your masters!'

'They isn't my masters any more, Winky!' said Dobby defiantly. 'Dobby doesn't care what they think anymore!'

'Oh, you is a bad elf, Dobby!' moaned Winky, tears leaking down her face once more. 'My poor Mr Crouch, what is he doing without Winky? He is needing me, he is needing my help! I is looking after the Crouches all my life, and my mother is doing it before me, and my grandmother is doing it before her. Oh what is they saying if they knew Winky was freed. Oh the shame, the shame!' She buried her face in her hankie and bawled.

'Winky,' said Hermione, firmly. 'I'm quite sure Mr Crouch is getting along perfectly well without you. We've seen him you know –'

'You is seeing my master?' said Winky breathlessly, raising her tear

stained face out of her skirt once more, and goggling at Hermione.
'You is seeing him here at Hogwarts?'
'Yes' said Hermione. 'He and Mr Bagman are judges in the Triwizard Tournament.'
'Mr Bagman comes too?' squeaked Winky, and to Harry's great surprise she looked angry again. 'Mr Bagman is a bad wizard! A very bad wizard! My master isn't liking him, oh no, not at all!'
'Bagman – bad?' said Harry.
'Oh yes,' Winky said, nodding her head furiously. 'My master is telling Winky some things! But Winky is not saying. Winky – Winky keeps her master's secrets . . .'
She dissolved yet again in tears; they could hear her sobbing into her skirt. 'Poor master, poor master, no Winky to help him no more!!'

From **The Goblet of Fire** by J.K. Rowling (Bloomsbury, 2000)

What did you think about Winky? Work with a partner and draw a mindmap with Winky's name at the centre. Around Winky's name write down as many words as you can to describe the kind of 'person' she is. Now work with another pair. Show them your words and explain to them what evidence you found in the passage that made you pick these words.

Look at the way J.K. Rowling makes Winky speak. What are the differences between the way Winky speaks and the way Hermione speaks?

You could say that Winky is speaking like all the other elves. We could say that Winky and Dobby are speaking in an elvish dialect, whereas Harry and Hermione are speaking in Standard English.

When would *you* use dialect and when would you use Standard English?

Whether we like it or not, people make assumptions about the kind of people we are, from the way we speak and write. If we want to be in control, we have to think carefully about:

- what we say

- how we say it

- the most appropriate language for our audience.

If we choose the wrong dialect people might make assumptions about us. They might think we are stupid, or they might not be able to understand us.

Here is a piece of poetry written in the dialect of Shetland and another piece written in Glasgow dialect. In each of these areas people would enjoy reading words in their own dialect, but what would the problems be if each had to read – and try to understand – the dialect of the other?

Shetland dialect

I' da dim, saft simmer hom.
  Dere, A'm pluckin kokkiluries,
  An gadderin paddick-stols,
  Or guddlin tricky skeeticks
  Ida clear saat-waater pols,
  A'm rickin peerie sillicks
  Wi a preen an dockin-waand
  Or pokin efter smislins
Ida ebb-stanes ida saand.

From 'Shetlan' by John Peterson in **The Kist/A Chiste** (Nelson Blackie, 1996)

Glasgow dialect

See you?
– ye daighie
   ye dummeral
   ye gowkish, glaikit gommeral
– see you? What are ye?
A noofie nyaff
A sair mishanter
A ginkie gyte
A chanty wrastler
A mingin mess
A fousome fogel
A yella yite
A tattie-bogel!

From '*See You?*' by Donald Campbell in **The Kist/A Chiste** (Nelson Blackie, 1996)

You know the difference between dialects now, so it's up to you to make your own language choices.

- Who would think you are too posh if you spoke Standard English?

- Who would look down on you if you didn't?

- Are there any circumstances, e.g. a family wedding or a funeral, when both are used at different times?

Verb – to give

I <u>gave</u>	I have <u>given</u>
You <u>gave</u>	You have <u>given</u>
He/she/it <u>gave</u>	He/she/it **has** <u>given</u>
We <u>gave</u>	We have <u>given</u>
They <u>gave</u>	They have <u>given</u>

You should work at getting these forms right, particularly in your writing, but also in your speech.

> **An easy way to remember which form to use is that the form with the 'have' ends in the sound 'n' (see<u>n</u>, do<u>n</u>e, go<u>n</u>e, give<u>n</u>).**

There are a number of other words which vary like this. Though they are not used so frequently, you should still try to get them right.

Verb	Past Tenses		
	Form 1		**Form 2**
To draw	I <u>drew</u>	but	I have <u>drawn</u>
To fall	I <u>fell</u>	but	I have <u>fallen</u>
To eat	I <u>ate</u>	but	I have <u>eaten</u>
To drive	I <u>drove</u>	but	I have <u>driven</u>
To ride	I <u>rode</u>	but	I have <u>ridden</u>
To rise	I <u>rose</u>	but	I have <u>risen</u>
To take	I <u>took</u>	but	I have <u>taken</u>
To write	I <u>wrote</u>	but	I have <u>written</u>
To fly	I <u>flew</u>	but	I have <u>flown</u>
To go	I <u>went</u>	but	I have <u>gone</u>

> **Note that for these words, the 'n' sound rule still applies.**

There are a few words where the change is not so drastic, but you still need to know the correct form.

Verb	Past tenses	
	Form 1	Form 2
To begin	I <u>began</u>	I have <u>begun</u>
To drink	I <u>drank</u>	I have <u>drunk</u>
To ring	I <u>rang</u>	I have <u>rung</u>
To shrink	I <u>shrank</u>	I have <u>shrunk</u>
To sing	I <u>sang</u>	I have <u>sung</u>
To sink	I <u>sank</u>	I have <u>sunk</u>
To spring	I <u>sprang</u>	I have <u>sprung</u>
To stink	I <u>stank</u>	I have <u>stunk</u>
To swim	I <u>swam</u>	I have <u>swum</u>

And finally, two oddities:

To come	I <u>came</u>	I have <u>come</u>
To run	I <u>ran</u>	I have <u>run</u>

You may think that it doesn't matter whether you get these right or not since you do not, at present, need them to impress an employer or bank manager. But what about your teacher, headteacher, dentist, doctor or any other person whom you want to think highly of you? And thinking about the long term, it's easier to sort out these things now so that, in future, you don't need to be watching every word when it *does* matter.

You will be confident that no-one is laughing at you because you have said:

'I seen it lots of times.' *When you should say:*

'I have seen it lots of times.' *Or* 'I saw it last week.'

23 Unlocking writing: it's not what you write, it's the way that you write it

What do you need to know about language? You actually already know a great deal about language and how it is used. However, you possibly don't know many of the jargon words that will help you to talk and think about the way you and other people use language.

If you really want to be good at unlocking text, it will help if you learn some jargon. This isn't hard.

What is jargon? Everything has its own jargon. These are special words which people 'in the know' use, and which mean that they are immediately understood by others who are also 'in the know'. It's a bit like being a member of an exclusive club. Only those who are members know the words to use. Like these words and phrases from football and computing:

- Free kick

- Hard disk

- Memory

- Offside

- URL

- Corner kick

- UEFA

- Close the window

These terms might not mean anything to someone who has never played football or worked at a computer, but they are instantly recognisable to those who have.

Think about a hobby or an interest that you have (a sport, a pastime, a type of music). It will have its own special language. You are going to find out if your partner knows the jargon for your specialist area. Put the name of your specialist subject in the centre of a spidergram and brainstorm as many jargon words as you can. Swap your brainstorm with a partner and see if they understand what the terms mean. Try to make it hard for them!

What has this to do with unlocking the text?

There are jargon words in English language too and, if you know them, you will be able to understand what texts are about, how they work and how the writer is trying to influence you. You will also find it easier to discuss your work with others and with your teacher. As a result, you will be able to communicate better – this is the point of the exercise.

Choosing the best words

We are going to read a passage from a book called *Skellig* by David Almond. In the story, the main character, a boy, has just moved into a new house. There is a tumble-down garage in the garden and the boy is convinced that there is something strange at the very back of the garage. In this extract, he goes into the garage for the second time and he is determined to find out who . . . or what is there.

As you read, try to think about the atmosphere the author is trying to create and how he does this.

Don't worry about the highlighting for the moment. We will explain later.

Something little and black scuttled across the floor. The door creaked and cracked for a moment before it was still. Dust poured through the torch beam. Something scratched and scratched in a corner. I tiptoed further in and felt spider webs breaking on my brow. Everything was packed in tight – ancient furniture, kitchen units, rolled-up carpets, pipes and crates and planks. I kept ducking down under the hose pipes and ropes and kit bags that hung from the roof. More cobwebs snapped on my clothes and skin. The floor was broken and crumbly. I opened a cupboard an inch, shone the torch in and saw a million woodlice scattering away. I peered down into a great stone jar and saw the bones of some little animal that had died in there. Dead bluebottles were everywhere. There were ancient newspapers and magazines. I shone the torch on to one and saw it came from nearly fifty years ago. I moved so carefully. I was scared. I was scared every moment that the whole thing was going to collapse. There was dust clogging my throat and nose. I knew they'd be yelling for me soon and I knew I'd better get out. I leaned across a heap of tea chests and shone the torch into the space behind and that's when I saw him.

I thought he was dead. He was sitting with his legs stretched out, and his head tipped back against the wall. He was covered in dust and webs like everything else and his face was thin and pale. Dead bluebottles were scattered on his hair and shoulders. I shone the torch on his white face and his black suit.

From **Skellig** by David Almond (Hodder Children's Books, 1998)

So, what kind of atmosphere is the author trying to create? What picture is he trying to transfer from his head into ours?

Discuss this in pairs and then report back to the class.

We think that David Almond wants to build up suspense. He describes the setting in order to create an atmosphere that is chaotic, old, neglected, dry and dusty.

Let's look at how he does this.

Work in pairs and underline anything which the boy can **see**, **touch**, **taste**, **smell** or **hear** that creates this chaotic, old, neglected, dry and dusty atmosphere and which is slightly scary.

Compare what you have underlined with another pair.

You will probably find that David Almond has chosen the objects he describes very carefully. In other words, he will have chosen his **nouns** very carefully. This is a jargon word which you need to know

What is a **noun**?

A **noun** is a label that we attach to things so that we know what they are. It can be something you can see and touch:

- door
- dust
- carpets
- pipes
- crates.

Or it can be something you can't see or touch, but it still needs a label to give it a name. Think how the boy in the story was feeling. He might have felt:

- fear
- anxiety
- regret
- anger.

Look again at David Almond's writing. This time highlight in red any **nouns** he uses. We have done some for you to give you a start. Why do you think the author particularly used these nouns? Why does he use so many nouns? Why does he make lists of them?

Work with a partner and make two columns in your jotter. Put the heading 'nouns' in the left-hand column. Leave the second column blank for the moment. Pick out the nouns the author has used which help to reinforce the idea that the atmosphere is dry, dusty, slightly sinister and pretty chaotic.

Let's look at his sentences to see what we can 'unlock'.

Look at these examples. What effect is he trying to create in each case?

> **I moved so carefully. I was scared. I was scared every moment that the whole thing was going to collapse.**

What about these sentences? Do they have a different purpose?

> **Everything was packed in tight – ancient furniture, kitchen units, rolled-up carpets, pipes and crates and planks. I kept ducking down under the hose pipes and ropes and kit bags that hung from the roof.**

Can you see how the author varies the lengths of his sentences? Sometimes they are very short and sometimes they are much longer. Why does he do this?

Starting a sentence

Look at how David Almond begins his sentences:

- *I tiptoed further in …*
- *I kept ducking down …*
- *I opened a cupboard an inch …*

It could get boring if every single sentence began in this way, so then he changes the pattern:

- *More cobwebs snapped on my clothes and skin.*

Work with a partner and see if you can spot any other changes to the pattern '**I** did this. **I** did that.'

Sometimes the author repeats words. Which words does he repeat? Why does he do this?

Some sentences are long lists of objects. Read these sentences out loud. Better still, ask your partner to read them out loud. Listen hard. What kind of effect do you think Almond was trying to create?

Writing challenge

David Almond used particular words – nouns, verbs and adjectives to create an atmosphere. He used different lengths of sentences to build suspense and to keep us interested. You have now unlocked that text, learning that by choosing particular words you can create a particular effect.

As a writer, you have to decide on your audience and what the purpose of your writing is before you begin. Think what kind of atmosphere you are going to create and then choose your words and sentences carefully to help you communicate with your reader.

Now it's your turn. You are going to create a short piece of text for someone else to unlock. Imagine you are scared, so scared that you have run off somewhere to hide. Where might that be? It could be somewhere very cold and damp, slimey and smelly. Try to picture it and to feel what it might be like. Use all of your senses – touch, taste, sight, sound and smell. How do you feel?

page 17

Think of small details which will help your reader to imagine the scene. Remember you want to show you are scared and to create an atmosphere that is full of suspense. Your reader needs to be able to see exactly what is in your mind. Your challenge is to create a word picture which gets this over to your reader. Remember to use some of the techniques David Almond uses. Choose your words carefully. Use the best nouns, adjectives and verbs you can think of.

More about words

Here is another passage for you to talk about and to unlock. In Jacqueline Wilson's *Girls Under Pressure*, Ellie, the main character, is worried about being fat. She diets and diets, but still feels fat. Later Ellie goes to the psychiatric ward to visit another girl, Zoe, who has been admitted to hospital as she is suffering from anorexia. Ellie cannot find Zoe but as she is walking through the ward of other anorexic girls, Jacqueline Wilson, the author, describes what Ellie can see and what she thinks. As you read, try to think what Jacqueline Wilson wants you to feel about anorexia.

It's as if it's another planet peopled by a strange new sisterhood. **Painfully** thin girls are sitting watching television, dancing **jerkily** to pop music, exercising in baggy tracksuits, flicking through magazines, huddling in high-necked sweaters, crying in corners. It's not just their skeletal state that makes them look alike. They've all got withdrawn absorbed expressions on their faces as if they're watching television screens inside their own heads. Even when they talk to each other they have a zombie look. It's like they're all under the same enchanted spell.

For one moment it works on me too. I look **enviously** at their high cheekbones and fragile wrists and colt-like knees, feeling **grotesquely** fat and lumbering in their ethereal presence. But then a nurse walks past carrying a tray – a **lively** looking young woman with shiny bobbed hair and a curvy waist and a spring to her step. She's not thin, she's not fat, she's just a **normally** nourished healthy person. I look at her and then I look at all the anorexic patients.

I see them **clearly**. I see their thin, lank hair, their pale, spotty skin, their sunken cheeks, their sad, stick limbs, the skeletal, inward curve of their hips, the ugly spikiness of their elbows, their hunched posture. I see the full haunted horror of their illness.

From *Girls Under Pressure* by Jacqueline Wilson (Corgi Books, 1998)

Make a table with three columns this time: nouns, verbs and adjectives. Pick out these particular words from the passage and talk about whether you think they are used effectively or not. Remember to think about the *purpose* Jacqueline Wilson had in writing like this. Do the nouns, verbs and adjectives she chose help her to put her point over to the reader?

Adjectives	Nouns	Verbs

Adverbs

Another term you need to know, because it is useful for seeing what Jacqueline Wilson is trying to do is **Adverb**.

An adverb is a word or phrase (small group of words) which tells you more about the verb. Authors use them to make their writing more interesting by telling you how, when or where the action happened. The following examples have adverbs in purple.

Adverbs can tell you *how* something happened:

- They were dancing jerkily
- Ellie spoke quietly.

Adverbs can tell you *where* something happened:

- The nurse came here.

Adverbs can tell you *when* something happened.

- The doctor will come tomorrow

Adverbs are often placed next to their verb, but they can also be found in different parts of the sentence. Where the author puts the adverb can make a difference to the meaning of the sentence. Have a look at the sentences below.

In which sentence is Ellie walking home *most* slowly?

- Ellie walked slowly home.
- Ellie walked home slowly.
- Slowly, Ellie walked home.

Adverbs often, but not always, end in –ly

- quickly
- slowly
- smoothly
- quietly.

Sometimes an adverb gives you more information about an adjective ... The girl was painfully thin.

Painfully tells you just how thin she was.

Adverbs are usually used a bit more sparingly than adjectives as they can make the writing seem overdone rather than interesting; a bit like eating too many Mars bars at one sitting.

Some adverbs that Jacqueline Wilson uses are written in purple in the text.

We use metaphors all the time without even thinking about it. We talk about:

- going ballistic

- letting off steam

- blowing a fuse

- being cool.

What do these sayings really mean? Why do you think they are used so much?

Can you think of any other metaphors and similes which we use in everyday life? Maybe you could make a wall display of everyday metaphors and similes. Think of those connected with being angry, with how time passes or the weather. You could add regularly to your collection.

Now you have an idea about how similes and metaphors can be used to create a clear word picture in our minds. You have also learned two more technical or **jargon** words. Well done!

Writing challenges

1 Imagine Miss Honey walks along the corridor on her way to her classroom. Describe her and give her something to do that shows that she is a very different kettle of fish from Miss Trunchbull.

2 After you looked at *Skellig*, you wrote some text about a setting where you were hiding. You used adjectives and nouns carefully to describe the scene. Now you could put characters into that setting. Why are they there? What do they look like? What do you want your readers to think about them?

3 Now give them something quite simple to do which shows something about the kind of people they are. Think about using one or two adverbs, a simile or a metaphor. Don't overdo it or you will spoil the effect you are trying to create.

4 If you like, you could continue your story. What problem or conflict are you going to set up which needs to be resolved?

24 Showing your best face: unlocking presentation

Punctuation

Do you think that punctuation is something that teachers invented just to annoy you?

Try reading a bit of the *Skellig* passage without any punctuation and see if you can work out what punctuation is for.

i keep ducking down under the hose pipes and ropes and kit bags that hung from the roof more cobwebs snapped on my clothes and skin the floor was broken and crumbly i opened a cupboard an inch shone the torch in and saw a million woodlice scattering away i peered into a great stone jar and saw the bones of some little animal that had died in there dead bluebottles were everywhere

Work with a partner and read it out loud. You might have to keep stopping and starting, and rereading parts before you can get it to make sense. How boring would it be if we had to do this with everything we had to read?

This exercise should help you work out what punctuation *is* for?

Discuss this issue with your partner and then with the whole class.

Remember to punctuate your own work as it helps your reader to understand what you are trying to say. Reading your writing out loud to a partner might help you to decide what punctuation to use.

To understand the *Skellig* passage you would put in full stops and capitals. That is because it is just simple narrative.

But the minute we write anything more complicated, we need much more punctuation to get it to make sense. How many different kinds of punctuation can you find in the passage on the next page, from the start of a book on the Loch Ness monster? Draw a table like the one that follows and say how each form of punctuation helps the reader to make sense of the account. Finally, name them or get your teacher to name them. The first two are done for you.

Glossary

Full stop (Sometimes called a period)
A single dot used to show the end of a sentence. Now also used to mark off items in a website address.

Capital (letter)
Used for the first letter of a new sentence or for proper nouns.

Punctuation mark	How it helps	Name
–	It makes a definite break in the sentence so that we look at the two parts quite separately.	dash
,	It makes the reader pause and realise that another point is about to be made.	comma

Here is the extract for you to look at.

Loch Ness is one of the most famous tourist sites in the world – not simply because of its stunning beauty, but mostly because of the mystery of the 'Monster' that may lurk in its waters. Known affectionately as 'Nessie', this elusive creature has been chased with great zeal for most of the 20th century, and this enthusiasm shows no sign of diminishing.

A monster at Loch Ness was first chronicled in AD 565, in an episode concerning the Irish missionary – Saint Columba. According to his biographer, St Adamnan (who wrote a century afterwards), one of St Columba's disciples was swimming across the River Ness to fetch a boat for his master. Suddenly, a monster broke the surface, 'with a great roar and open mouth'. Not unnaturally, the onlookers were 'stricken with great terror', but St Columba made the sign of the cross, saying: "Think not to go further, nor touch thou that man. Quick, go back . . ."

The creature obeyed. The saint's intervention seems to have been extraordinarily effective, for in the 1400 intervening years, the monster has not only refrained from attacking any of its dozens of witnesses, but has been remarkably silent. It roars no more.

From **The Loch Ness Monster** by Lynn Picknett (Pitkin Unichrome)

In fact, each bit of punctuation can be used for several purposes, but the ones we want you to recognise are shown in the table below.

Punctuation mark	What it does	Name
,	Makes us pause when reading so that we don't run one idea into the next. Used to separate the items in a list.	comma
'...'	Often used when the writer wants to quote from someone else's writing.	Single inverted commas
"..."	Used when the writer wants to represent the actual words spoken by someone (direct speech).	Double inverted commas
(...) or – ... –	Used to stick in an afterthought or bit of additional information which is not strictly a part of the original sentence.	parenthesis or brackets
's	Used to indicate possession, i.e. that the object following the 's belongs to the person or thing.	apostrophes
Capitals, but not at the beginning of the sentence	Used at the beginning of names for people and places and special one-off objects like book titles.	capitals

Punctuation mark	What it does	Name
:	Used sometimes to introduce direct speech (see extract on page 152). Used to tell us that what follows is an explanation for, or elaboration of, the first part of the sentence.	colon
;	Used to separate items in a list when the items need several words to say what they are. Used to separate two parts of a sentence when each part is very important or different from the other part.	semicolon
-	Used to link two closely associated names, objects or ideas.	hyphen

Here's another extract from *The Loch Ness Monster*. Look just at the colon and semicolons.

We have listed above two uses for each. Which uses of the colon and the semicolon appears in the extract?

'Writing in 1924, John Lockhart said in his *Mysteries of the Sea*, 'most of the witnesses [to the sea-serpent] agree on its outstanding features: it is a long serpentine creature; it has a series of humps; its head is rather like a horse's; its colour is dark on top and light below; it moves by undulations up and down; it appears during the summer months . . . it is harmless, for it never actually attacks anybody.' Presumably the serpent had learnt better manners since the days of Aristotle!

Use this section for reference when you are trying to understand a writer's use of punctuation; or when you are trying to punctuate your own work.

It may also give you ideas for putting together new kinds of sentences of your own.

25 Unlocking presentation: showing your best face

Layout

The way a **text** is laid out on the page is very important. Bring in some texts to look at. Why are they laid out in particular ways?

You could examine:

- calendars
- adverts
- junk mail
- food wrappers
- bills
- greetings cards
- menus
- programmes (theatre or football)
- comics
- fanzines
- poems.

Different texts are laid out in a particular way so that we can tell at a glance exactly what kind of texts they are. You could make a collection of text types. Produce a wall display showing similarities and differences in layout in different kinds of text.

Fonts

Many people now use computers to make their own texts and they can choose from different **fonts**. A **font** is the shape of a letter produced by a computer. Fonts can give different **messages** too.

In each of the signs opposite there is something wrong, not in the wording, but in the choice of font which has been used. The font is not suitable for the **purpose** and the **audience**. Say what is wrong with each one?

Computers
Expertly repaired

Danger
Do not touch

INVITATION
Please come to a party

Olde English
Furniture
Expertly repaired

The same words can give different messages depending on the fonts used. A company has sent out a reminder that a customer owes them some money. The customer has ignored the reminder, so the company sends out another and another. The words are the same but the message is becoming stronger. Work out the order in which the reminders were sent.

This account is overdue.
Please send in your payment

This account is overdue.
Please send in your payment

This account is overdue.
Please send in your payment

This account is overdue.
Please send in your payment

Layout can be particularly important in poetry.

Look at the poem on the next page by Benjamin Zephaniah. Why do you think BZ used these particular fonts?

ACCORDING TO MY MOOD

I have *poetic* **licence**, i WriTe thE way i waNt.
i *drop* my **full stops** where *i* like ---
MY CAPITAL Lete**R**s go where i li**KE**,
i **order** from **MY** PeN, i verse **the way** I like
(i do *my spelling write*)

Acording to My *MO*od.
i **HA**ve Poetic **licence**,
i put my **commers** where **i** like,,((O).
(((my brackets *are* **write**((
I REPEAT **WH**en i lik**E**.
i can't **go rong.**
i *look* and **i.c.**
It's rite.
i**l** REPEAT **WH**en i lik**E** **i have**
poetic **licence**!
don't question me**?? ??**

From **Talking Turkeys** by Benjamin Zephaniah (Puffin, 1995)

Some other layout challenges

1 Look at this extract from *Holes* by Louis Sachar. Why do you think he laid out his passage like this?

There is no lake at Camp Green Lake. There once was a very large lake here, the largest lake in Texas. That was over a hundred years ago. Now it is just a dry, flat wasteland.

There used to be a town of Green Lake as well. The town shrivelled and dried up along with the lake, and the people who lived there.

During the summer the daytime temperature hovers around ninety-five degrees in the shade – if you can find any shade. There's not much shade in a big dry lake.

The only trees are two old oaks on the eastern edge of the 'lake'. A hammock is stretched between the two trees, and a log cabin stands behind that.

The campers are forbidden to lie in the hammock. It belongs to the Warden. The Warden owns the shade.

Out on the lake, rattlesnakes and scorpions find shade under rocks and the holes dug by the campers.

Here's a good rule to remember about rattlesnakes and scorpions: if you don't bother them, they won't bother you.

Usually.

Being bitten by a scorpion or even a rattlesnake is not the worst thing that can happen to you. You won't die.

Usually.

Sometimes a camper will try to be bitten by a scorpion, or even a small rattlesnake. Then he will go to spend a day or two recovering in his tent, instead of having to dig a hole out on the lake.

But you don't want to be bitten by a yellow-spotted lizard. That's the worst thing that can happen to you. You will die a slow and painful death.

Always.

If you get bitten by a yellow-spotted lizard, you might as well go into the shade of the oak trees and lie in the hammock.

There is nothing anyone can do to you anymore.

From Holes by Louis Sachar (Random House, 2001)

page 39

2 Look at the work you did on found poems. What decisions did you make about layout there. Now you know a bit more about layout, would you do anything differently?

Here is another Benjamin Zephaniah poem you might like. Look at the layout and fonts he uses here. Why do you think he has done this? Maybe it was just for fun!

For Word Thank You

Thank you for the *words* I read
Thank you for the **words** I need
Thank you for the WORDS so great
Thanks for *words* that raise debate,
Thanks for the **words** on my bookshelf
Thanx for the **words** I make myself
Thank you for words that make me cry
And words that leave me feeling dry.

Thanks for WORDS that do inspire
And those words that burn like fire
Thanks for all the **words** I note
Thank you for all the *words* I quote,
I thank you for the **words** like me
Thanks for *WORDS* that set me free
And I thank you for *words* like you
I always need a word or two.

Thanks for **words** that make things plain
And words that help me to explain
Thanks for **words** that make life fun
And *words* that help me overcome,
Thanks for **words** that make me rap
Thanks for *words* that make me clap
Thanks for WORDS that make me smile
Thanks for WORDS with grace and style.

Thanks for all those **words** that sing
Thanks for **words** are everything
Thanks for all the **WORDS** like this
And little sloppy *words* like kiss,
Thanks for words like hip-hooray
And those cool **words** I like to say
Thanks for *words* that reach and touch
Thank you very, very much.

For Word Thank You by Benjamin Zephaniah from The Puffin Book of Utterly
Brilliant Poems (Puffin, 1999)

Glossary

These are our simple explanations of complicated ideas. Words in orange are explained elsewhere in the Glossary. Talk about this Glossary and its explanations with your teacher. Make your own Glossary.

Abbreviation: a shortened form of a longer word sometimes reduced to initials, e.g DJ for disc jockey.

Accent: a distinctive way of pronouncing words often associated with a region, a country, or part of a country, e.g. American accent, Aberdonian accent, etc.

Acronym: a word made up of the first letters of other words which represent the object.

Adverb: a word that tells us more about a verb or adjective.

Adjective: a word that describes a noun or pronoun.

Aerial or long shot: in film making this shot is taken from above. It lets us see everything that is going on.

Alliteration: repeating the same sound for effect, e.g. Lucky Lottery.

Appropriate: suited to, in line with, what you would expect from this genre of text.

Argument: a discussion to support or oppose an idea.

Atmosphere: a feeling or mood which a place creates in us, e.g. of fear in a horror story.

Audience: the person or persons reading, watching or listening to a text (see target audience).

Autobiography: the story of a person's life, told by him or herself.

Backlight: the main source of lighting in this case comes from behind the subject being filmed or photographed, giving it the appearance of a shadow or silhouette.

Bias: not as strong as prejudice. Selection of information by someone who is inclined to favour one person or one side of an argument

Bilingual: able to speak, and write in two languages.

Biography: the story of a person's life told by someone else.

Blurb: usually appears on the cover of books. It is a brief introduction to the subject of the book.

Bold: a form of type with darkened lettering used to emphasise words (see italic).

Broadsheet: a category of newspaper which puts emphasis on accurate and level-headed reporting.

Browser: computer program for reading and moving between texts on the Web (see search engine).

Camera angle: the position of the camera in relation to what is being shot, e.g. from below makes the subject seem big and powerful.

Camera focus: in film-making, the use of a device to show some things clearly and others less clearly.

Capital letter: used always to mark the first letter of a new sentence and of proper nouns.

Caption: alongside newspaper and magazine photographs, this summarises or comments on what we are seeing.

Chair: the person who manages a meeting *and*, when a **verb**, performing *as* a chair.

Character: person or being in a **fictional text** *and/or*, his or her personality.

Characteristics: the features of someone or something which are similar to, or different from, others of the same type.

Cliche: **word**s or ideas that have become boring through overuse.

Close-up shot: in film making shows us the detail of a character's face or of an object, like a turning doorhandle.

Code: the features of something (like a type of photograph) which, once recognised, allow you to identify it.

Colloquialisms/slang: speech forms used in a written text.

Column: a block of print, several of which are lined up to form the page of a newspaper or magazine.

Common noun: a noun which is the name for an everyday object, person, feeling or idea, e.g. table, footballer, terror.

Communication: the exchange of **information** and feelings between individuals and groups.

Complex sentence: a sentence made up of one main statement and one or more other statements, joined to the main statement by words such as 'when', 'who', 'if'.

Compound sentence: a sentence of two or more statements of equal importance joined by 'and', 'but', or 'or'.

Conclusion: a final decision *or* the summing up of ideas in, or at the end of, a **text**.

Confrontation: the situation in which, in stories or real life, when two or more people meet, there is conflict.

Connotation: the analysis of the hidden significance of the items in a picture, poster, film frame or scene.

Context: all the aspects of a situation which are affecting the event being discussed.

Copy: used as a noun, it refers to text written for publication, e.g. by a newspaper or for a poster.

Data: pieces of information organised in some way for some purpose.

Deep focus: in film making when the camera lets the audience take in all aspects of the situation. The foreground and background are both clear.

Definition: an explanation of the meaning of a **word** or **image**.

Denotation: the identification of the contents of a picture, poster, film frame or scene.

Derivation: the word in another language from which the English or Scottish word came.

Description: an account of how something or someone looks.

Diagram: a drawing of something, *and/or* of a process, often showing how it/they work(s).

Dialect: (Also called a *variety*.) A language obviously different from related language in its **accent** or **word**s and their use, e.g. Doric is a dialect of Scots spoken in Aberdeenshire.

Dialogue: the words used by **characters** usually in **scripts** and **fiction** *and* a conversation between people.

Dictionary: a book listing **word**s in alphabetical order, giving their meanings, how they are said and sometimes their histories.

Directions: **information** on how to do something *or* to go somewhere.

Direct speech: quoting the actual words used and using inverted commas to identify them.

Draft: writing (usually) that is still being worked on; also used as a **verb**, e.g. she drafted the report in a few hours.

Edinburgh Book Festival: an annual event held in August, lasting two weeks and bringing together a wide variety of authors and readers.

Editing: the rewriting or reordering of **text**s such as print, audio or visual materials, and their parts, to improve them.

Editorial: a section of a newspaper, or some magazines, which represents the newspaper's views about one issue in the news.

English: the common **language** of the British Isles, spoken here and across the world with many **accent**s and in many **dialect**s, and descended mainly from the Old English found in southern and central England.

Establishing shot: used in film-making, it allows the audience to take in one of the characters and the situation they find themselves in.

Fiction: a form of made-up story usually based on imaginary events and **characters**.

Figurative language (also called *figure of speech*): **word**s used to describe something by means of, for example, **metaphor**s and **similes**.

Filler light: used in film-making to soften the glare and shadows produced by the **keylight**.

First person: used where the speaker or writer is referring to her or himself, using **word**s like I, me, mine, etc. (see **third person**).

Fonts: the particular design of the typeface used in printing a text.

Formal: following set rules.

Formal language: conforming to the rules of respected written language.

Found poem: a poem made up from selected words and phrases from another text.

Full-page spread: where columns are not used to form the page of a newspaper; the story is spread all across the page.

Full stop (also called a *period*): a mark of punctuation, a single dot, used to mark the end of a sentence. Now also used to separate items in a website address.

Gaelic: a Celtic language found mainly in Scotland and Ireland.

Genre: a particular type of writing or text which has features in common with others of the same type, e.g. in story genre we can expect to find a plot.

Image: usually a picture, such as a photograph; also a group of **word**s that make a picture in our imaginations.

Informal: relaxed, casual, not following rules (see **formal**).

Informal language: using casual forms of language, sometimes nearer to the spoken than to the respected written forms, e.g. 'don't' rather than 'do not'.

Information: knowledge transmitted *and/or* received, usually about a particular matter.

Instruction: a piece of **information** providing knowledge *and/or* understanding, usually about how to do something.

Internet: worldwide **information** highway made from inter-connected computer networks.

Introduction: the first or opening part of, for example, a **text**, e.g. a story, a speech, a film.

Italic: a form of type with *lightened* lettering sloping to the right used for emphasis or to show quotation (see **bold**).

Jargon: words used by particular groups to talk about an activity they, but not everyone, share.

Keylight: in film-making, this is usually the main light that lights the character or scene.

Language: the **communication** systems used in speech, writing, visual texts, etc.

Layout: how **text**s, or parts of texts, are set out on a page or screen.

Long shot: in film-making, this shot takes in the whole environment in which the action takes place.

Mass media: forms of **communication** that reach large numbers of people through e.g. books, newspapers, radio, television, films, music, the **Web**, etc.

Metaphor: when one thing is said to be another to help us imagine what is being described, e.g. when Tommy 'flamed' his rage is seen as a sudden eruption of fire.

Mid shot: in film making it takes in the character(s) in more detail so that we can now see clearly who they are and what they are doing.

Mise en scene: the way a single shot or short series of shots is planned on the filmset. It is exactly what the director decides to put into the shot(s).

Monologue: one person speaking, usually to an **audience**, in a play or poem.

Montage: in film-making, the sequence of shots once it is filmed and edited, and ready to be shown.

Mood: the **atmosphere** created in a text, e.g. happy, scary, sad.

Motives: the reasons why **characters** behave in certain ways e.g. because they are angry, hurt or frightened.

Movie still: a single frame from a film turned into a photograph.

Narrative: a **text** which tells a story, e.g. a **novel**, an opera, a TV soap opera.

Neologism: new, made up word.

Non-fiction: a **text**, usually written, dealing with facts, real people and events which actually happened (see **fiction**).

Non-standard variety: a form of language which, in Britain, is not **Standard English**.

Noun: the **word** used to describe a person, a place, an object, a feeling or quality, or a collection of things.

Novel: a long piece of **fiction** about the lives and experiences of a number of **characters** (see **short story**).

Onomatopoeia: where the sound of a **word** suggests its meaning, e.g. hush, roar, rumble.

Opinion: a person's belief or judgement on some issue.

Panning or tracking shot: in film making the camera swivels to move across the scene, so taking in all that is happening.

Paragraph: a group of **sentences** about the same topic, usually part of a longer, written **text**.

Past tense: the form of the verb which shows us that it refers to events which have already happened.

Personification: where an object or idea is spoken of as if it had human qualities, e.g. the wind moaned through the trees.

Perspective: viewpoint, point of view. 'Another perspective' means to look at something in a quite different way.

Phrase: a few words which make sense together but do not form a complete **sentence**, e.g. on the table.

Play: a piece of writing intended for performance by actors *and* the performance itself.

Plot: what happens in a story.

Plural: more than one.

Point of view: a person's, or **character's**, way of looking at things.

Prejudice: judgement or opinion which might not be based on facts. This is usually written by someone who has a definite sympathy or dislike for a person or idea.

Pronoun: a word standing in the place of a noun, e.g. I, me, her, him, it, etc.

Proofread: to read through a piece of writing, looking for mistakes to be corrected.

Proper noun: a noun beginning with a capital letter, which is the name of a particular person, object or place, e.g. Harry, Shetland, Treasure Island.

Punctuation: marks used in writing to show such things as pauses, **sentences** and how to say **words**, e.g. commas, full stops and exclamation marks.

Purpose: the main intention or reason for doing something.

Rastafarian: the Rastafarian religion originated in Africa. It is often associated with the poorer black population of Jamaica. It is not just a religion, but a way of life. Rastafarians speak out against poverty, oppression and inequality.

Recount: a type of narrative writing telling about past events.

Redraft: a piece of writing rewritten after **editing**; also used as a **verb** (see **draft**).

Reggae: a particular genre of music which originated in Jamaica in the 1960s.

Relationships: in life how people, and in **fiction** how **character**s, behave with one another.

Reported speech: giving an account of what was said but not using the actual words.

Rhyme: usually in poetry, when the last sound of a line (or, more rarely, a sound anywhere in the line) repeats one found earlier.

Rhythm: sound patterns made by regular emphasising of **word**s or **syllable**s or by adopting particular sentence structures, e.g. 'Know what I mean?' 'Not a soul.'

Scanning: reading a text carefully to find one particular piece of information.

Scene: a part of a **play** *and*, from this, an episode in e.g. a comic, **short story**, **novel** etc.

Scots: a **language** spoken in Scotland and Northern Ireland, descended mainly from the Northumbrian variety of Old English with, in its northern varieties, Old Norse.

Screivin: Scots for 'writing', can be a **noun** or **verb**.

Script: a written **text** usually meant to be performed by actors.

Search engine: program on the **Internet** allowing users to search for files and **information**.

Sentence: a group of **word**s begun with a capital letter, ended with a full stop, and usually a complete thought.

Setting: the place, and its conditions, where the **plot** happens in a **narrative text**.

Shallow focus: in film-making this technique makes the subject stand out sharply to catch your attention. Only the foreground can be seen clearly; the background is fuzzy.

Short story: a **text**, always **fiction**, of perhaps less than 1000 words, usually more (see **novel**).

Simile: **figurative language** in which one thing is said to be *like* or *as* another, e.g. he's *like* a zombie watchin yon telly.

Sign: a simple public notice, with or without words, carrying a message, e.g. a street name or road sign.

Simple sentence: a sentence with only one statement.

Singular: the term describing one-ness.

Skimming: reading a text quickly to gain the gist of the passage.

Slang: **words** in a special language invented to meet the needs of a group.

Slogan: a short phrase or statement designed to catch people's attention and sum up a more complex set of ideas or circumstances.

Soap opera: a serial, usually on radio or television, chiefly concerned with emotions of regular characters. Originally sponsored by soap powder manufacturers.

Soft focus: in film making, using special lenses or filters to soften the lines of the subject

Source: the place, person or organisation which originally supplied the information.

Standard English: a **dialect** of **English** written and spoken in a common (i.e. 'standard') form across the British Isles – and elsewhere – but spoken with many **accents**.

Style: the ways a writer or talker uses **language** for a particular effect.

Subject: the person, or topic, at the centre of a **text** or some form of enquiry, or the **word** in a sentence with which the verb agrees.

Subheading: titles used to mark sections of a newspaper story or chapter of a book and to say what the coming section is about.

Summarise: to pick out and put together in your own words the main points of a text.

Syllable: one of the sounds that make a **word**, thus in Auchterarder, *auch*, *ter*, *ard* and *er* are all syllables.

Symbol: a sign or object which stands for something, e.g. the logo on your trainers which represents the company which makes them.

Target audience: the particular **audience** at which a **text** is being aimed.

Teaser poster: poster put out in advance of a film's release, to create interest.

Text: any made thing which conveys **information**, e.g. writing, picture, recorded conversation, sound, etc.

Theme: a main matter with which a **text** is concerned, e.g. love, hatred, youth, age, etc.

Third person: used where the speaker or writer is referring to others e.g. she, her, he, him, it, they, them etc. (see **first person**).

Tone: the feeling or mood expressed by the speaker or writer of a text.

Topic: a subject about which to talk or write.

Tracking shot: used in film-making where the camera follows a moving person or object.

Trailer: an extract from a film or TV show, shown in advance and designed to whet your appetite.

Trilingual: able to speak and write in three languages.

Typeface: the shape of the letters used in printing and publishing texts or on a computer.

URL: (Uniform Resource Locator) an **Internet** address, e.g. the URL for ***Turnstones*** is http://www.turnstones-online.co.uk

Verb: the **word** in a **sentence** that shows movement, action, or conditions.

Verse: lines in a poem that form an obvious group on the page.

Visualise: to picture the scene in your mind.

Voice: sounds produced by the vocal organs *and* how **words** are uttered in a **text** or by a person.

Word: the basic unit of language: in writing and sometimes speech, separated from others by spacing.

Web: the World Wide Web, WWW in **URLs** – inter-linked sites on the **Internet**, their **text**s read by means of a **browser** and entered with **URLs.**